THE ROMANCE OF AMERICAN TRANSPORTATION

THE ROMANCE OF AMERICAN TRANSPORTATION

Revised Edition

by FRANKLIN M. RECK

AVA MORGAN, *Picture Editor*

Thomas Y. Crowell Company : New York

Designed by Ava Morgan
Manufactured in the United States of America
Library of Congress Catalog Card No. 62–18235
ISBN: 0-690-71033-X
Published in Canada by Fitzhenry & Whiteside Limited, Toronto.
5 6 7 8 9 10

CONTENTS

Harper's Magazine, 1889

Washington met by his neighbors on his way to the inauguration.

I · IN 1789

IN APRIL, 1789, when George Washington set out from Mount Vernon for New York, to be inaugurated as first President of the United States, a trip from one city to another was an adventure.

There were no surfaced highways between towns. The road over which Washington traveled was a narrow, winding, rutted track. Here and there, farmers had thrown rocks into the trail to make a surface, but this merely made the road more bumpy and treacherous. A writer of the day protested indignantly that it took five days to travel one hundred miles from Baltimore to Philadelphia, and that the road was in such dangerous condition that coaches were frequently overturned and passengers killed.

The coaches that passed Washington as he rode north were plain wagons with heavy leather side curtains to let down in case of rain. Inside were four or five benches without backs. The passenger entered the coach at the front and crawled over crowded seats to find a vacant place at the rear. A man was lucky to get a ride in one of the newer coaches in which the seats rested on springs. The comfortable Concord coach with its upholstered seats and outside rack for luggage hadn't yet been invented.

Brown Brothers

Washington's own coach wasn't much better than the public vehicles of the day, and for that reason he took along his favorite saddle horse. Thus, when the jolting and swaying of the coach proved too much for him, he could gain a measure of relief by riding his horse.

In order to get from Baltimore to New York in a week, the citizens of Washington's day had to get up at dawn and travel until after dark, with an occasional stop at a tavern to change horses and refresh themselves. To make time, the coachman galloped his horses downhill, risking his own neck and those of his passengers.

Hudson Historical Bureau

Boston Post Road at Union Square, New York, in 1822.

As the coach careened along the narrow road, it would often tip perilously. When it was about to sway to the right, the driver would call out, "To the left!" and all the passengers would throw their weight to the left to help keep the coach on its wheels. Furthermore, whenever the coach got stuck in the mud, all able-bodied passengers were expected to get out and push. An intercity trip, in 1789, was likely to combine the thrills of a modern-day roller coaster ride with a considerable amount of backbreaking labor.

Travel in 1789 wasn't cheap. The fare from Philadelphia to Baltimore was $6.25, with lodging and meals at the taverns extra. Between Boston and New York the cost was $10.00 by stage, tavern expense extra, and $8.00 by sailing packet, meals included. In view of the low salaries of the time, these rates can be considered fairly costly.

It's surprising how little communication there was in 1789 between the large cities of the seaboard. From New York to Boston and from

Worcester Historical Society

"The Unrivaled Express Rider" carried dispatches from Worcester, Massachusetts, to Hartford, Connecticut: sixty-six miles in three hours and twenty minutes.

New York to Philadelphia, mail went three times a week in summer and twice a week in winter. It was carried by horseback, and two saddlebags per trip sufficed to transport all the letters that people were writing in those days.

Much of this must have been on Washington's mind as he rode north that April to take charge of a new nation. He himself was a great traveler, perhaps one of the most widely traveled men in the entire country. At sixteen he had gone into the valley of the Shenandoah to survey the lands of Lord Fairfax, and he had been out to the Ohio region several times. Few people knew the country better than he, and nobody realized more keenly how important it was to bind the young country closer together with better transportation.

Here was a nation of four million people, thickly settled along the seaboard and extending barely 250 miles inland at any point. Many of the citizens of the big eastern cities were showing a restless tendency to go west.

Some families were making their way by wagon and pack train along the Mohawk Valley in upper New York state, while others were taking the trail over the Catskills into southern New York.

They were following the rivers, too. Poling their belongings upstream by flatboat, whole communities were following the Susquehanna River into the interior of Pennsylvania.

From Virginia and North Carolina, settlers were entering Kentucky by Daniel Boone's Wilderness Road, and from eastern Georgia other settlers were trickling northwest into the valley of the Tennessee River.

From Baltimore, more families were traveling on the old Braddock Road toward the Ohio River, there to build rafts and float down the Ohio until they found a likely piece of farm land not too close to the Indians. The Braddock Road was the only real highway to the west. This widened trail, hewn through the wilderness to permit passage to General Braddock's supply wagons, had been built for war purposes, like the roads of Caesar in Gaul, but now it was carrying peaceful settlers into lands of promise—and hardship.

Thin trickles of humanity traveling west by a half-dozen routes, only one of which could be called a road. The trickle was like the leakage from a weakening dam before it bursts, a warning of the flood of humanity that was to go billowing and roaring across the continent, inundating America from Atlantic to Pacific in the brief span of one hundred years.

Already, in 1789, 170,000 citizens of the United States were living

beyond the Alleghenies, and this scattered group worried George Washington. They needed roads so that they could trade with the cities of the eastern seaboard. As it was now, they were forced to pack their furs and hides across the mountains on the backs of horses and mules. Because it didn't pay to ship bulky grain by pack horse, they converted the grain into whiskey and then shipped it to the East in that form.

If Ohioans wished to sell their cattle in the East, they were faced with the necessity of driving overland along trails that had originally been laid out by the buffalo and then used by Indians. The three-hundred-mile journey took months and the cattle arrived at the coast gaunt and hungry. In the very farm lands south of Philadelphia through which Washington was riding were pastures where Ohio cattle were fattened before they were brought to market.

If these Ohio settlers didn't get roads, there was no knowing what they would do. They might even ally themselves with Spain, for Spain still controlled the Mississippi River, and Washington knew that Spain hadn't given up her hope of establishing an empire on this continent. It was far easier for Ohio and Kentucky settlers to load their grain, lumber, and cattle aboard flatboats and float them down to Spanish New Orleans than to attempt to haul them over the mountains. For lack of transportation, the United States might lose the country beyond the mountains.

There was something heroic about travel and trade in 1789. It was heroic to drive cattle hundreds of miles on foot, in order to sell them in Philadelphia and Baltimore. It took personal courage to attempt a stagecoach trip from Boston to Philadelphia. It required a high order of hope and self-confidence for a man to load his wife and children and few belongings aboard a flatboat and start poling it upstream into the wilderness. But these methods of travel reveal just how primitive our country was on the day it inaugurated its first President.

The United States in 1789 was a slumbering young giant, its coal mines mostly undiscovered, its iron mines barely scratched, its forests still standing as they had stood for a thousand years.

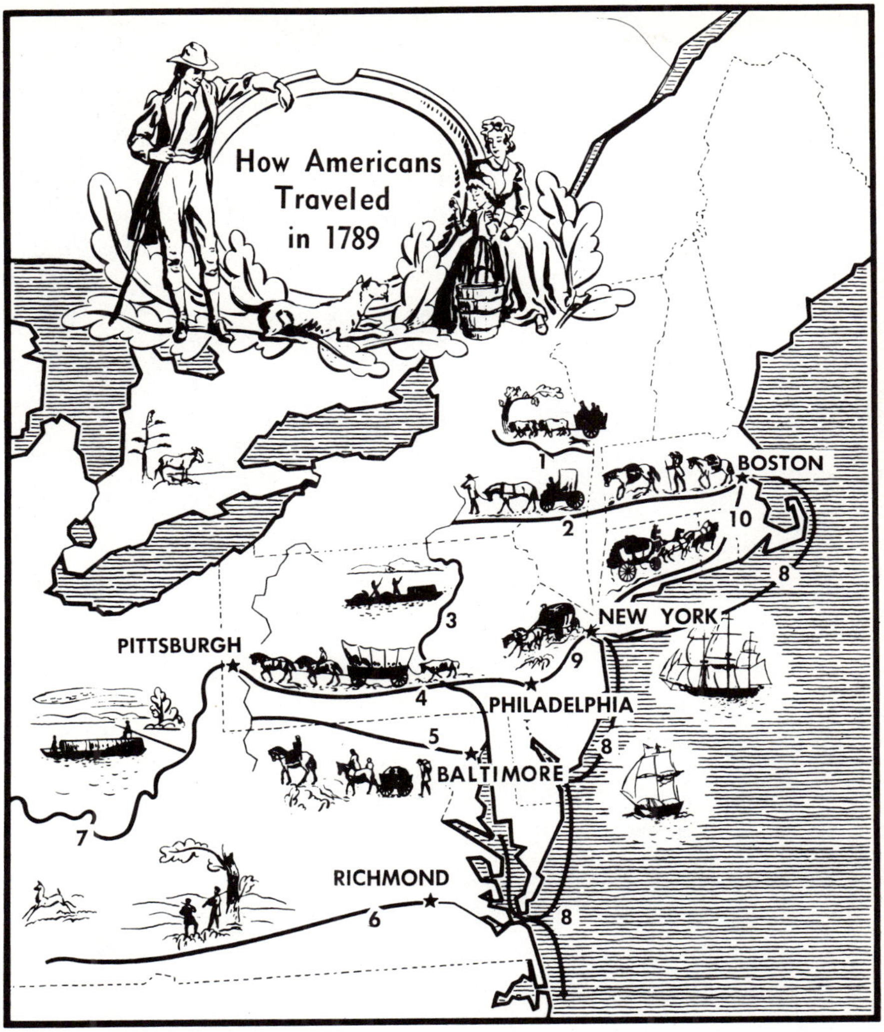

1 · Westward along Mohawk Valley by wagon and pack train
2 · Westward via the Catskills by wagon and pack train into lower New York
3 · Poling barges up the Susquehanna to clear land in Pennsylvania
4 · Philadelphia to Pittsburgh by Conestoga wagon
5 · Baltimore to the Monongahela by wagon and pack train
6 · Boone's Wilderness Trail from Richmond to Kentucky
7 · Floating down the Ohio on flatboats
8 · Coastwise sailing boats
9 · Stagecoaches from New York to Philadelphia
10 · Stagecoaches from New York to Boston

Emmet Collection, New York Public Library

Brooklyn, New York, 1776.

There were no factories. There were only a few steam engines in the entire country.

Yet things were happening that April, as Washington bumped and swayed toward New York. The nation's transportation system was dimly forming in men's minds. The seeds of the modern era were sprouting in the fertile imaginations of a few dreamers.

On the waters of the Delaware at Philadelphia, even as Washington approached that city, the ragged, half-starved John Fitch was struggling with an experimental steamboat, and could point with pride to the fact that it had already made several runs of five miles per hour against the current.

In the same city, at that same time, an acquaintance of John Fitch's, an engineer named Oliver Evans, was planning to put a steam engine on a boat-shaped wagon and operate it both on the highway and on water, thereby creating an amphibious automobile.

Here and there, forward-looking men were talking about building canals around the rapids of rivers, so that boats could go farther inland. Washington himself was interested in a plan to build a canal around the rapids of the Potomac.

Other men, owners of quarries and mines, were struggling toward the beginnings of a railroad system, wondering if they couldn't lay rails of wood a mile or two from their mines to the nearest river. They could build these plank rails just far enough apart so that wagon wheels would rest on them, thus enabling horses to draw greater loads with less work than over the bumpy, rutted trails.

London Magazine, 1764

A coal wagon which ran on rails between the mines and the ships. The front wheels were of iron and the back wheels of wood.

The wealthy John Stevens, later to be called the "father of the railroad," was studying steam engines on his Hoboken estate.

All this in April, 1789. The steamboat, canal system, railroad, and automobile had their shadowy beginnings as Washington traveled in his coach up the highway from Wilmington to Philadelphia, on his way to New York. People were even taking to the air! Only six years earlier, the Montgolfier brothers had built large paper-and-silk balloons, filled them with hot air by building a fire beneath them, and sent them up with passengers aboard at Annonay, France.

A New England town in 1800.

We have presented these brief facts to give a bird's-eye view of the nation as it was at the dawn of its transportation era. In addition, another event was taking place in 1789 and 1790—an event of greatest importance to the story of transportation in the United States:

In 1789 an Englishman just twenty-one years of age named Samuel Slater took passage for America to build cotton-spinning machinery. He had served as apprentice and overseer in an English textile factory and felt sure he could reproduce the machines in this country. He was not allowed to bring plans with him, because England was jealous of her growing manufactures and did not intend to let any other nation usurp the business.

So Slater came without drawings. But, at the falls of the Pawtucket River in Rhode Island, from memory he constructed a complete spinning mill. He superintended the building of the mill, taught Americans to operate it, and our first mass production factory was on its way.

But a mass production factory is of no use without cheap and swift transportation. There is no point in manufacturing more cotton cloth than your own locality can use if you cannot conveniently ship the surplus elsewhere and sell it.

The United States in 1789, with manufacturing about to start, with forests waiting to be cut and mines to be opened, with settlers going west in increasing numbers—this young nation needed transportation far more than even Washington realized.

To provide that transportation, Fitch, Evans, and Stevens were clutching at dim ideas . . . puffing steamboats on the rivers and inland lakes . . . long ditches filled with water along which barges and packets glided, drawn by mules and horses . . . wooden rails—perhaps iron rails—on which horse-drawn wagons operated . . . wagons propelled by steam, rolling along the highway with no horse in front of them. . . .

Washington could not have prophesied just what shape these dim ideas would take as he rode north through the blossom-scented orchards of southern Pennsylvania to take the oath of office as first President of the United States, that April day in 1789.

Brown Brothers

Fitch's experimental steamboat on the Delaware River, at Philadelphia, in 1786.

2 · JOHN FITCH - THE STORY OF A MAN

WASHINGTON had shown an interest in better roads, the improvement of river navigation, and even the steamboat, but after he took office he had little time to devote to these matters. His task was to set up a new and untried government, and such practical matters as transportation were perforce to be left to individuals. One of these individuals was John Fitch.

A year after George Washington took over the government in New York, John Fitch reached his hour of greatest triumph and greatest despair. Early in the summer of 1790, after four years of experiment and public ridicule, he put into operation between Philadelphia and Trenton the first regular steamship service to be established in the United States.

His boat was forty-five feet long, which is about two-thirds the length of a present-day railroad coach. Amidships stood a fire-box and an iron boiler. A cylinder with a diameter of twelve inches supplied power to a set of paddles at the rear of the boat. Forward of the tall smokestack stood a small cabin for passengers. The boat could make eight miles an hour.

The papers announced that "The Steamboat" would leave Arch Street in Philadelphia three times a week and carry passengers to Trenton, forty miles away, for five shillings—about $1.25. To encourage the public to try this new means of travel, free beverages and sausage would be served in the cabin.

The Steam-Boat

IS now ready to take Paſſengers, and is intended to ſet off from Arch ſtreet Ferry in Philadelphia every *Monday, Wedneſday* and *Friday,* for *Burlington, Briſtol, Bordentown* and *Trenton,* to return on *Tueſdays, Thurſdays* and *Saturdays*—Price for Paſſengers, 2/6 to Burlington and Briſtol, 3/9 to Bordentown, 5ſ. to Trenton. June 14. tu.th ftf

During the summer of 1790 the boat made at least thirty-one trips totaling more than a thousand miles. It went eighty miles in one day. It had no breakdowns that took more than an hour or two to repair. It went at least two miles an hour faster than Fulton's *Clermont* was to go in 1807.

Yet, with every trip "The Steamboat" lost money. Fitch's backers grew discouraged and withdrew their support, and the line discontinued its runs. Why was it that this magnificent early effort went down to failure? To answer that question we must go back a few years.

John Fitch began experimenting with steamboats on the Delaware in 1786. At that time, according to one authority, there were only three steam engines in the United States, and these were all stationary engines. To the citizens of this country the term "steam engine" was a vague and distant term.

Fitch knew that steam engines existed but that was all. He followed his own inspiration without help. His first idea was to apply steam power to wagons, but he decided no steam engine could pull a wagon through two feet of sticky clay in rainy weather. Boats were different. It would be fairly easy to propel a boat over the smooth, flat surface of a river. If the roads had not been so poor in 1786, Fitch might have been our first automobile maker.

Fitch had mechanical ability and great determination. He was born January 21, 1743, on a rocky farm near Windsor, Connecticut, and from earliest childhood his life was a story of hardships and thwarted hopes. What little formal schooling he enjoyed ended at the age of ten.

In his late teens he became apprenticed to a watchmaker, but the watchmaker used him on household chores and refused to teach him the trade. That was the first of Fitch's many disappointments.

As a young man without a trade, he wandered down to Trenton, New Jersey, where he made and peddled silver buckles. He taught himself to repair clocks, and picked up a few dollars that way. During the Revolution he fitted bayonets to guns and in the latter part of the war sold supplies to American troops.

Toward the end of the war, he walked out to Fort Pitt, floated down the Ohio on a raft, entered Kentucky at Salt River, and surveyed some good farm land there. Then he walked back to Richmond, Virginia, and recorded the land, hoping to get rich some day by selling the land to settlers.

In 1783–84 he made a trip to Ohio country to survey land for a group of Philadelphia men. While there he traced a map of the western country, and when he returned to Philadelphia he engraved the map on a copper plate and began selling it.

By this time Fitch had walked over that part of the United States embraced in a square running from Connecticut to Detroit to Kentucky to Virginia. He had seen with his own eyes the lakes and the rivers that formed a natural network of highways over the land, and it is not surprising that the idea of steamboats should occur to him.

Like every other inventor he began by building a model. He constructed a skiff two feet long, on each side of which he rigged two sprocket wheels with an endless chain running over them. Fixed to the endless chain were vertical paddles, like fins. These would engage the water in endless procession and drive the skiff forward. He tried the model in a small stream and it worked to perfection. Now, if he could build a large boat and apply steam for power, he had it!

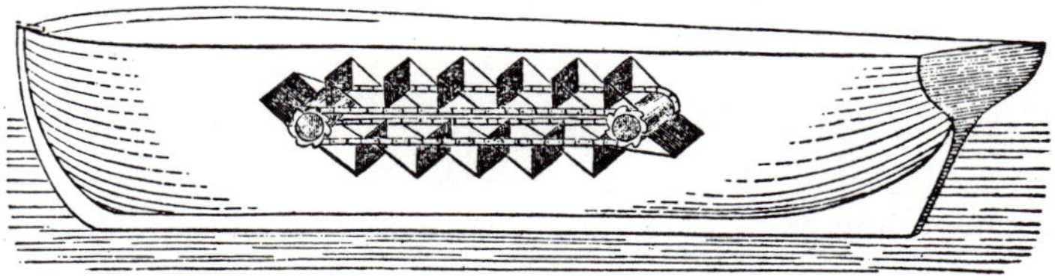

Old engraving

John Fitch's model of September, 1785, with endless chain, floats, and paddle boards.

With great hope he started out to get approval for the idea. For it took money to build boats and engines, and Fitch had no money. All he had was a burning conviction that would not let him sleep.

He submitted his dream to Benjamin Franklin, George Washington, and to Congress and received no more than polite nods. Undismayed, he began besieging various state legislatures for the exclusive right to build and operate vessels propelled by steam on the waters of the state. Finally New Jersey granted him the privilege he sought, doubtless with the idea that it is better to humor a madman than enrage him.

Armed with the New Jersey grant, Fitch succeeded in getting a group of Philadelphians of moderate means to contribute three hundred dollars toward the building of the first experimental boat. Next, he found a watchmaker named Henry Voight, a grumpy, competent man, to help him with the mechanical end.

It might have been better for Fitch's peace of mind had he never made this first start, for he was now to experience the jeers and ridicule that come to a man who proposes ideas that are too strange and bizarre for the public to accept.

With Voight he built a man-sized skiff equipped with his endless chains and paddles, and one spring day in 1786 he launched the skiff on the Delaware. There was no engine in the boat. He planned to turn the contraption with cranks, to see if it would really work.

A group of idlers—sailors and water-front men—lined the shore and grinned as Fitch and Voight shoved off. Fitch began turning the cranks and the skiff whirled first one way and then the other. For mechanical reasons that have not come down to us, the boat was unmanageable and the crowd on shore roared with laughter every time the craft performed a new gyration. There was only one thing to do—drop the crank handles, take up the oars, and row back to shore.

The moment they landed, Voight shoved off through the crowd, red-faced and angry. Why had he ever let Fitch talk him into helping with this crazy scheme? As for Fitch, he went straight to his room and did not appear again for two days.

But Fitch came out from his bedroom with a new idea. If the chain-and-sprocket idea was wrong, he would rig a set of oars along each side of the boat. These oars could be placed vertically on a sort of framework. Then it would be possible to actuate them by a set of cranks so that they would plunge into the water, take a stroke, lift themselves out of water, and swing forward for another stroke.

With eager enthusiasm Fitch went to Voight, and soon the two were working on their second boat. They built a shop model that worked to perfection, then applied the idea to the skiff. This time they installed a small steam engine which they had built themselves in Voight's shop.

In July, 1786, they launched the skiff and Voight fed hickory sticks into the firebox. The steam pressure mounted and the piston began moving. The oars—six on each side of the boat—began cleaving the water in strong, regular strokes.

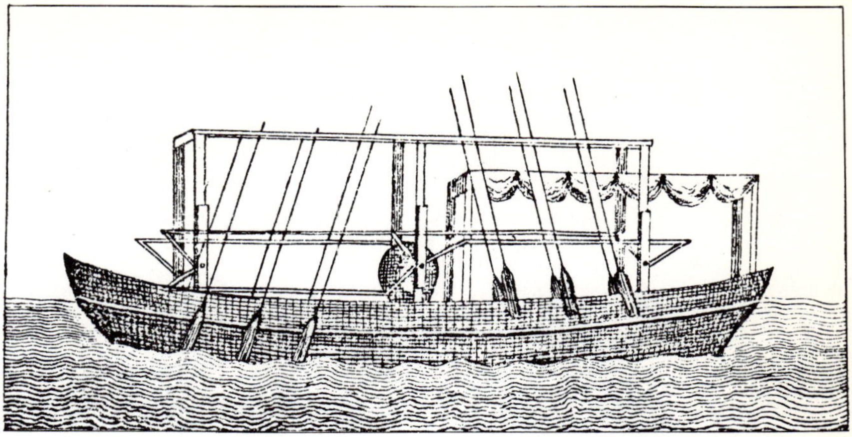

Plan for Fitch's steamboat.

Columbian Magazine, 1786

It must have looked strange to the spectators. With its twelve vertical oars, the boat was more like an ungainly water bug than anything intended for human use. No wonder the onlookers laughed once more.

But Fitch and Voight didn't mind. Their device worked, and now all they had to do was build a larger boat. Fitch began walking again —to Delaware, New York, and Virginia. When he returned, tucked in his ragged pocket was the exclusive right to operate steam vessels in all those states—and in his own state of Pennsylvania, as well.

With these grants he was able to raise more money, with the result that in June, 1787, the larger boat was finished and ready for trial. The Constitutional Convention was assembling in Philadelphia at the time and nearly every famous leader of the Revolution was there, but most of them were interested in far more weighty matters than steamboats.

This new boat was forty feet long, with a beam of eleven feet and a draught of three feet eight inches. The engine had a piston twelve inches in diameter and the big boiler was encased in bricks. Voight got up steam, and with several members of the Constitutional Convention aboard the boat moved out into the river.

The trial, on the whole, was disappointing. The boat made only two and a half miles per hour against the current, whereas Fitch had hoped for eight or ten. Worse yet, the rudder was too long and the boat was difficult to steer. At a bend in the river Fitch was unable to turn the craft in time and it became grounded in the mud. The guests aboard the boat shook their bewigged heads as they jumped off and went back to their lodgings.

The object of any trial is to discover the faults in an invention and correct them. This the two workers did, but money was scarce and the pathway these men followed was utterly new to mankind. It was a year later before they had a new craft ready to launch. In the interests of speed, this boat was slimmer. The entire engine had been taken down and made lighter. The brick around the boiler had been removed to save weight. The paddles had been placed in the rear of the boat where they would be more efficient.

By now, however, Fitch and Voight were the laughing stock of Philadelphia. In all this time Fitch had spent no money on clothes and very little on food. The solid citizens had seen him walking from shop to inn to water front, a gaunt, ragged specter. It is not surprising that they thought him more than a little crazy.

So, in July, 1788, when Fitch and Voight issued invitations for a trial trip in their rebuilt steamship, only two stockholders of the company had the courage to go aboard for the test trip which was to be all the way to Burlington, twenty miles up the river.

Voight tended the furnace and Fitch steered, as usual. The paddles in their framework at the rear of the boat lifted themselves, came forward, thrust themselves into the water, and moved back.

The boat got up speed. Leaving the shore with its grinning spectators behind, it forged into the current and created a ripple of waves. The minutes sped by and the neat houses of Philadelphia faded in the distance.

Fitch felt the thrill of speed. This boat was going faster than their previous one. Four miles an hour at least. Possibly five. He watched the countryside glide by. Miles dropped behind them and the boat never faltered.

Near Dunk's Ferry some of Fitch's loyal friends had obtained a brass cannon that had been used in the Revolution. As "The Steamboat" approached the ferry they touched off the cannon and a *boom* echoed over the water.

Far up the river Burlington crept into sight. Henry Voight became enthusiastic. He fed more and more wood into the furnace until the fire was a pounding inferno. Proudly America's only steamboat turned its prow toward the wharf where hundreds of people waited. Smoke poured out of the stack. The welcoming committee lifted a great cheer. Only a few hundred yards more . . .

Then something happened. There was a cracking noise and a white cloud of steam hissed from the boiler, enveloping the dismayed crew in its wet billows. The pressure dropped, the piston slowed down, then stopped altogether. The boat came to a stop, still some distance from shore, and began to drift backward with the current.

Fitch and Voight had made the boiler of insufficient strength and the seams had given way under the high pressure Voight had built up. There was no safety valve on the boiler. The inventors had never heard of a safety valve and, moreover, had not foreseen that it was possible to get up too much steam. Two men had toiled ceaselessly for two years, only to have a ridiculous accident turn their moment of triumph into comedy.

Again they corrected the boat's faults, and in the spring of 1790

Fitch's stern-paddle steamboat, 1788.

Hudson Historical Bureau

they launched the final version of their steamboat on the regular service described at the beginning of the chapter. Now, however, we can begin to understand why the steamboat failed to capture the public imagination.

For four years, "poor Johnny Fitch" had been the joke of the town. He was the fellow who was trying to run a boat with a teakettle. If anybody wanted a good laugh, all he had to do was go down to the Delaware shore and watch that lanky New Englander try to make his boat behave.

The good citizens of Philadelphia, Burlington, and Trenton knew what stagecoaches were. They were familiar with the sailing packets that operated up and down the river. But a wooden boat operated by fire—they couldn't dream of such a thing because they had never seen one before.

So John Fitch, who had created an entirely successful steamboat, who had met and overcome every mechanical fault that had presented itself, became a prophet crying in the wilderness.

In speaking of the importance of steam navigation, Fitch had written to Franklin: "It is a matter of the first magnitude not only to the United States but to every maritime power in the world . . . It will answer for sea voyages as well as for inland navigation."

To Congress he had petitioned: "The subscriber begs leave to lay at the feet of Congress an attempt to facilitate the internal navigation of the United States, adapted especially to the waters of the Mississippi."

To the Pennsylvania Assembly he had predicted that steam transportation would triple in value all the country northwest of the Ohio River by making it possible for these far westerners to send their produce down the Mississippi.

In his writings and declarations Fitch clearly foresaw the bustling days of Mississippi steamboating and oceanic travel, but he was almost alone in his vision. A contemporary, writing of Fitch and his company during those last days in Philadelphia, said:

"They (Fitch's backers) already rendered themselves the subjects of ridicule and derision for their temerity and presumption in giving countenance to this wild projector and visionary madman. The company thereupon gave up the ghost, the boat went to pieces, and Fitch became bankrupt and brokenhearted. Often have I seen him stalking about like a troubled specter, with downcast eye and lowering countenance, his coarse soiled linen peeping through the elbows of a tattered garment."

Wild projector . . . Visionary madman . . . Strange words to use in connection with a man whose only fault was that he saw the future with a clearer eye and a keener mind than his fellows!

There was one forlorn hope left for Fitch. A man who had become enthusiastic about Fitch's steamboat was, in 1793, an American consul in France. This man—his name was Aaron Vail—invited Fitch to come over to France and build steamboats there.

Fitch went, only to find that the people of France had just cut off the heads of their sovereigns, Louis XVI and Marie Antoinette. They were in the midst of a revolution and nobody was interested in steamboats.

Fitch's screw propeller steamboat, 1796.

The inventor returned to this country, fifty-one years old and disillusioned. He worked on the docks in Boston, wandered down to New York and built a small steamboat operated with a screw propeller, similar in general idea to the ocean liners of today.

Nobody, apparently, paid much attention to it. At any rate, Fitch left New York and walked out to Kentucky, only to find that the lands he had so carefully surveyed and registered were overrun with squatters who refused to recognize his title to them.

He induced a lawyer to take up the matter for him, then went to an innkeeper at Bardstown, Kentucky, with a proposal.

"I've got some good farm lands around here," he said, "but I've got to prove my title. If you'll board and keep me, I'll give you half the lands."

The innkeeper accepted the proposal and Fitch puttered around and waited. He was ill and afflicted with pains and the doctor gave him pills to take one at a time. He saved these pills, and one night in the year 1798 he took them all at once, gulped down a swallow of water, and lay back on his cot.

They put him in an unmarked grave near the Ohio River, which was to become in forty years one of the great steamboat highways of the world.

There is one bit of evidence that Fitch's brilliant mind and agile fingers were still busy during those final days in Kentucky. There was found in his room a model steam engine three feet long, supported by flanged wheels under a rectangular truck. Can it be possible that he foresaw not only the era of steamboat travel, but the day of the railroad as well?

John Fitch's trouble was that of a star actor who walks on the stage in Act One, when he is not due until Act Two. Act One in the United States was devoted to the drama of a young nation showing that it could govern itself. A constitution had to be adopted and put into effect. Government bureaus had to be formed. An army, a navy, and a national bank had to be started.

The chief performers in Act One were George Washington, Alexander Hamilton, Thomas Jefferson—men who were playing with this new and fascinating idea of Democracy. Nobody quite realized the pressing need for swift boats that would go against the current as well as with it, thereby uniting all the lands that lay along the Great Lakes and the rivers into one great, prosperous trading community.

No one knew that a great man had walked among them and had ended his own life in bitterness out in Kentucky.

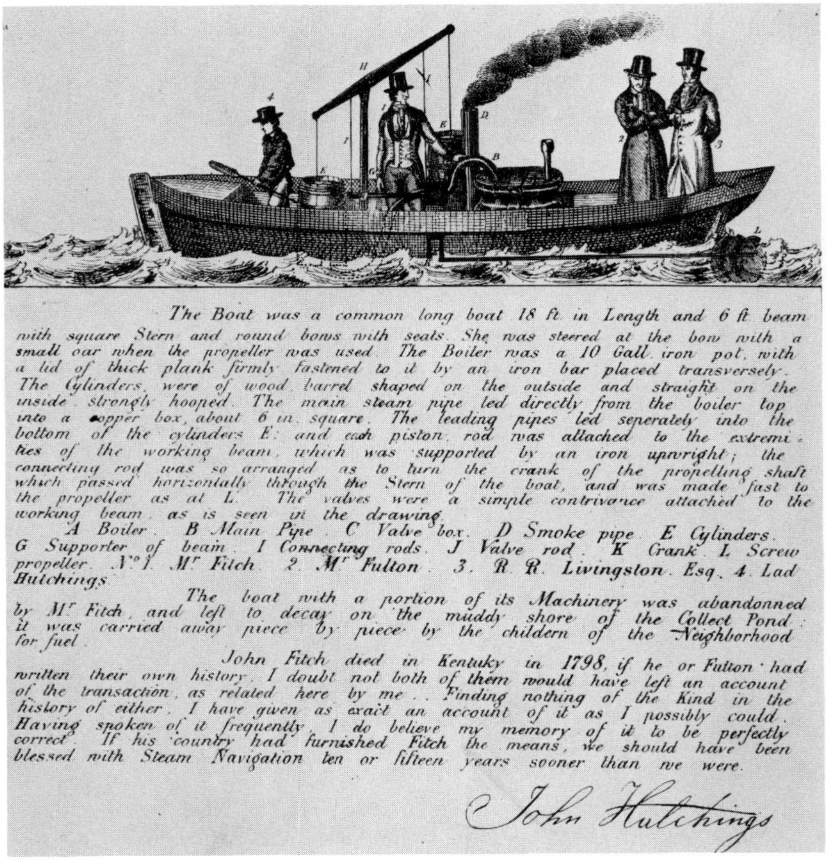

The Boat was a common long boat 18 ft. in Length and 6 ft. beam with square Stern and round bows with seats. She was steered at the bow with a small oar when the propeller was used. The Boiler was a 10 Gall. iron pot, with a lid of thick plank firmly fastened to it by an iron bar placed transversely. The Cylinders, were of wood, barrel shaped on the outside and straight on the inside. strongly hooped. The main steam pipe led directly from the boiler top into a copper box, about 6 in. square. The leading pipes led seperately into the bottom of the cylinders E: and each piston rod was attached to the extremities of the working beam, which was supported by an iron upright; the connecting rod was so arranged as to turn the crank of the propelling shaft which passed horizontally through the Stern of the boat, and was made fast to the propeller as at L. The valves were a simple contrivance attached to the working beam, as is seen in the drawing.

A Boiler. B Main Pipe. C Valve box. D Smoke pipe. E Cylinders. G Supporter of beam. I Connecting rods. J Valve rod. K Crank. L Screw propeller. N.° 1. M.r Fitch. 2. M.r Fulton. 3. R. R. Livingston. Esq. 4. Lad Hutchings.

The boat with a portion of its Machinery was abandonned by M.r Fitch, and left to decay on the muddy shore of the Collect Pond: it was carried away piece by piece by the childern of the Neighborhood for fuel.

John Fitch died in Kentuky in 1798, if he or Fulton had written their own history, I doubt not both of them would have left an account of the transaction, as related here by me.. Finding nothing of the Kind in the history of either, I have given as exact an account of it as I possibly could. Having spoken of it frequently, I do believe my memory of it to be perfectly correct. If his country had furnished Fitch the means, we should have been blessed with Steam Navigation ten or fifteen years sooner than we were.

John Hutchings

Fitch's last boat was operated by a screw propeller like the ocean liners of today. This account by an eyewitness tells how it was left to rot.

The steamboat in the center is the *Clermont*. The caption refers to it as "the first steamboat," although Fitch had successfully operated steamboats twenty years earlier.

3 · ROBERT FULTON – THE STORY OF A STEAMBOAT

In no sense can Robert Fulton be called the inventor of the steamboat. Rather, he is the man who took the inventions and devices of others and combined them into the first commercially successful steamboat in the world.

When we read in our histories that in 1807 the *Clermont* made its maiden voyage from New York to Albany and back, we are likely to think that the builder, after a few months of secretive labor, unveiled to the world an undreamed-of miracle. This is so far from the truth that it will pay us to trace the train of events that led to the building of the *Clermont*. It is not a connected story. Rather it is like the clues picked up by a detective and put together to form a pattern.

The first clue is found in Lancaster County, Pennsylvania, where Fulton was born in 1765. A friend of Fulton's family, William Henry, had built a steamboat model and tried it out in a small stream. As a boy, Fulton had doubtless first heard the strange word "steamboat" used in connection with Henry's experiment.

But Fulton, as a young man, was not primarily interested in steamboats. He was interested in art. In 1786, when John Fitch was beginning his experiments on the Delaware River, Fulton was a miniature painter in Philadelphia, living only a few minutes' walk from the river front where Fitch's experimental skiff was moored. Whether Fulton showed any interest in it or not, nobody seems to know. But he must have heard it discussed.

The clues that follow are indirect. Fulton went to England in 1786 to study art under the American painter, Benjamin West, who was then living in England. But England was just swinging into the industrial age. Watt was making steam engines, and Arkwright and Crompton were operating textile factories. In this atmosphere Fulton's interest in art waned and his interest in engineering grew. Such devices as a machine for twisting hemp into rope, a machine for sawing marble, and a plan for raising and lowering canal boats over an inclined plane engaged his attention.

More important, during these years when Fulton was turning to mechanics, English inventors built and operated at least five experimental steamboats, and it is known that Fulton talked to one of them —a Lord Stanhope.

Then comes a definite clue linking Fulton to Fitch. In 1788 a Virginia man named James Rumsey came to England. Rumsey had written a pamphlet on steamboats and was conversant with all of Fitch's work. Fulton and Rumsey spent considerable time together, and it is reasonable to suppose that Fulton learned the story of Fitch's mistakes and successive attempts to correct them.

From this point on we must follow a new trail—a trail that starts in the United States and leads to the Seine River, in Paris.

Stimulated by Fitch's heroic work, a number of Americans began experimenting with steamboats in the 1790's. The most significant one, from our standpoint, is Samuel Morey, who ran a stern-wheeler from Hartford, Connecticut, to New York, in 1794, making five miles per hour.

One of the men who inspected this boat was Robert R. Livingston, chancellor of the state of New York, the man who had administered the oath of office to George Washington in 1789. Livingston was a

Robert R. Livingston.
Hudson Historical Bureau

man of vision. He must have thought, as he rode on Morey's boat from New York to Greenwich, Connecticut, that here was an idea which would not die. Steamboats were the coming thing. And if they were the coming thing, why would it not be a good idea to obtain from New York the monopoly that had been granted to Fitch some years before?

So Livingston induced the state to revoke Fitch's monopoly and give it to him, on condition that he build a boat capable of making four miles an hour. He built the boat in 1798, but since it made only three miles an hour, the monopoly lapsed.

In 1801, Livingston was appointed United States Minister to the Court of Napoleon in France, and in this year the trails of Fulton and Livingston joined. Fulton was in Paris trying to interest Napoleon in his newest hobby, a submarine that actually submerged itself in the Seine, moved about under water, and rose again.

Fulton was considered by everybody a brilliant young man. His time was his own. Livingston, who was more determined than ever to build steamboats, went to Fulton. The result of their conversations was an agreement whereby Livingston was to advance £500 ($2,500) and Fulton was to build a trial boat on the Seine.

The trial boat, on the whole, was not successful. Fulton built the first hull too weak and it broke in two, sinking to the bottom of the Seine. The rebuilt boat, with a steam engine installed, was tried out on the Seine on August 9, 1803, and made a speed of only three and one-half miles an hour.

After this experience, Fulton decided to inspect the work of others. He took a short trip in a Scotch boat and made sketches of its machinery. He visited the consul, Aaron Vail, who had induced Fitch to come to France ten years before. Fulton borrowed Fitch's plans and kept them for several months. Finally, very wisely, he ordered a twenty-four horsepower steam engine from the foremost engine builders in the world, Boulton and Watt of England.

That completes the pattern of clues behind the building of the *Clermont*. Isolated facts, many of them, but they show that the genius of many men went into the building of America's first commercially successful steamboat. Fulton's contribution was in selecting the best of what others had done, adding his own ideas, and combining them in one craft.

The boat was tested on the East River on August 9, 1807, and began its historic trip to Albany at one o'clock on Monday afternoon, August 17. Forty men—investors in the company, Livingston and Fulton and their friends—stood in groups on the deck as the boat left its moorings in North River, near State's Prison.

Thousands of people lined the shore, craned their necks from windows, and sat perched upon the housetops—a far different audience from the water-front loafers and sailors who had jeered at the labors of Johnny Fitch and Henry Voight in Philadelphia. This immense New York crowd had heard about steamboats for seventeen years. They had read about one experiment after another. Their minds had changed from skepticism to doubt, and now, as the boat chuffed out into the Hudson, black smoke pouring from its thirty-foot stack, the last doubt disappeared and a roar of enthusiasm tumbled over the waters.

Here is the exact itinerary of that first voyage. The boat arrived at Clermont-on-the-Hudson, Chancellor Livingston's home 110 miles up the river, at one o'clock, just twenty-four hours after leaving New York. There the boat moored overnight—Tuesday night.

Wednesday morning at nine it left Clermont and arrived in Albany at five in the afternoon, going the forty-plus miles in eight hours. The total running time upstream was thirty-two hours, meaning that the boat had maintained an average speed of five miles per hour against the current.

Thursday morning at nine the boat left Albany, arriving at Clermont at six o'clock. An hour later it departed, arriving in New York at four on Friday morning. The running time downstream, thirty hours.

Although the boat must have appeared both awesome and magnificent to those thunderstruck men and women who lined the shore, it was in reality rather crude. The machinery in the center of the boat was entirely uncovered. The paddle wheels were unprotected. There were no cabins and no guard rails to prevent one from falling overboard.

Clermont going up the Hudson River.

As is usual with trial trips, this first voyage indicated changes to be made, and for several weeks Fulton was busy lengthening the boat, putting in cabins and berths, and decking over the boiler. An accurate description of the *Clermont* as she appeared on her first commercial trip, September 4, follows:

Chicago Historical Society

Artist's sketch of the enlarged *Clermont.*

Her over-all length was 150 feet and her beam 13 feet. She displaced 100 tons of water. Her prow was 26 feet high, of which all but two feet was above the water line. The bottom of the boat was of yellow pine plank, 1.5 inches thick, tongued and grooved and set together with white lead. Floors of oak and spruce were laid across the slightly curving hull. Two masts rose from the deck so that sail could be used to augment the engine when the wind was favorable.

Twelve berths were installed for the first voyage and all of them were taken at seven dollars per person. One of the passengers on this first trip, a Judge John Q. Wilson, gives a further description of the boat.

The forepart was decked over to provide shelter for the crew. To enter the passengers' cabin in the afterpart of the ship, you went around to the stern and descended a hatchway just in front of the tiller. Thick, black smoke issued from the thirty-foot stack, and steam hissed from all joints of the engine. It is reported that a member of the crew, with a bucket of hot lead, went around soldering up the cracks wherever he found steam escaping.

When the boat failed to leave on time, that September morning, one of the passengers asked anxiously if anything was wrong, and Fulton replied:

"Gentlemen, you need not be uneasy; you shall be in Albany before twelve o'clock tomorrow."

The boat pulled away at 6:42 a.m. before another great crowd. As a tremendous cheer shattered the air, one passenger observed that Fulton's eyes seemed to flash with unearthly brilliance as he drew himself up to his full height. He must have been an impressive man. He is described as over six feet tall, slender, energetic, with curly brown hair scattered about his forehead and falling to his neck. His forehead was high, his nose straight and prominent. He wore a white, loosely tied cravat, ruffles at his breast and sleeve, and left his waistcoat unbuttoned. What a picture he must have made in that hour of blinding glory.

Before winter set in that year, the boat, its accommodations enlarged, embarked with as many as ninety paying passengers.

Robert Fulton receives his first steamboat fare.
Hudson Historical Bureau

Since the expense of running the boat was not much more than twenty-five dollars a day, and a single passenger paid seven dollars for his ticket to Albany, it can be understood why the venture was considered profitable from the start.

The enlarged *Clermont* had a fore cabin containing sixteen berths, a great cabin with twenty-four berths, and a back cabin for ladies with twelve berths. Overflow passengers were accommodated on sofas. The regulations forbade passengers to go to bed with their shoes on, sit on tables, or smoke in any cabin except the fore cabin.

The age of the steamboat was under way.

Car of Neptune, 1809.

4 · THE FIRST STEAMBOAT ON THE MISSISSIPPI

LIVINGSTON and Fulton didn't stop with the building of the *Clermont*. In 1809 they built their second Hudson River boat, the *Car of Neptune,* 175 feet long and costing $25,000, and had a third boat under construction. Then they turned their eyes toward the west.

One of their partners was a man named Nicholas Roosevelt, grand-uncle of Theodore Roosevelt, President of the United States ninety years later. In 1809, Nicholas Roosevelt and his wife took a flatboat from Pittsburgh to New Orleans to see whether the Ohio and the Mississippi were suitable for steamboat navigation. His report to the New York partners was a glowing one, and as a result the company obtained from the territory of Louisiana the exclusive right to operate steamboats on the waters of the Mississippi. In 1810 Roosevelt was

New Orleans waterfront in 1803. Within twenty-five years the shoreline would be crowded with steamboats.

sent with workmen and machinery to Pittsburgh to build the first steamboat beyond the mountains.

Pittsburgh, of course, had heard about steamboats. Since 1794 they had had a stationary steam engine in the town. Undoubtedly many of its five thousand citizens, during visits east, had seen the *Clermont* churning up the Hudson. But the Hudson with its deep wide channel was different from the Ohio and the Mississippi with their rapids and snags and sandbars. Roosevelt, they decided, didn't know what he was facing.

Undaunted, Roosevelt went ahead with his little shipyard at the foot of Boyd's Hill, on the Allegheny side of town. Timbers for the boat's hull and cabins were cut from the near-by forests. A Boulton and Watt steam engine from England, carefully covered, waited to be installed. The Pittsburgh citizens of 1810 who were privileged to look at the Watt steam engine were unbelieving. Roosevelt was saying that this bulky contraption of iron would actually drive a boat *against* the current. Huh!

Roosevelt's project was the smallest part of the shipbuilding activity of the town. Here at Pittsburgh were built the flatboats, keelboats, and barges that floated down the river carrying the trade of the country between Pennsylvania and New Orleans. At Pittsburgh emigrant families loaded their entire possessions aboard flatboats—farm machinery, cows and chickens, furniture—and let the current carry them to a likely piece of land.

Barges loaded with salt pork, flour, fruit, cider, and lard were shoved out into the current never to return. Once at their destination and the supplies sold, some of the barges were broken up and the lumber sold for what it would bring. Then the bargemen would walk all the way back to Pittsburgh for the next trip. Across from New Orleans a town was constructed almost entirely of lumber from broken-up barges and flatboats.

Some boats were constructed with keels—a four-by-four beam of wood running along the bottom of the boat to take up the shock of collision. These craft, built with pointed bows, were used both upstream and down. They were driven upstream by shoving long poles into the bottom and pushing, or by towing from the bank with a long rope. And sails helped when the wind was following.

Crossing the Mississippi on ice.

Old print

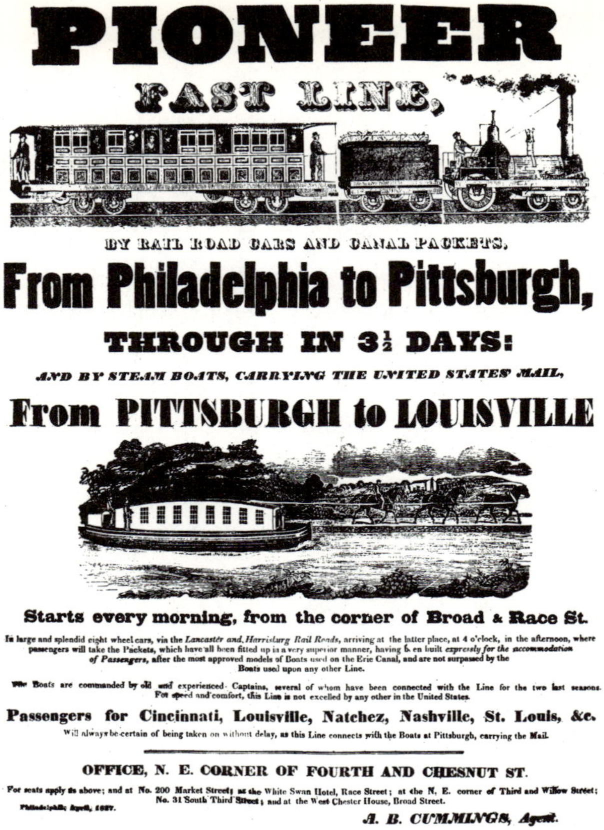

PIONEER

FAST LINE,

BY RAIL ROAD CARS AND CANAL PACKETS,

From Philadelphia to Pittsburgh,

THROUGH IN 3½ DAYS:

AND BY STEAM BOATS, CARRYING THE UNITED STATES MAIL,

From PITTSBURGH to LOUISVILLE

Starts every morning, from the corner of Broad & Race St.

In large and splendid eight wheel cars, via the *Lancaster and Harrisburg Rail Roads*, arriving at the latter place, at 4 o'clock, in the afternoon, where passengers will take the Packets, which have all been fitted up in a very superior manner, having been built *expressly for the accommodation of Passengers*, after the most approved models of Boats used on the Erie Canal, and are not surpassed by the Boats used upon any other Line.

The Boats are commanded by old and experienced Captains, several of whom have been connected with the Line for the two last seasons. For speed and comfort, this Line is not excelled by any other in the United States.

Passengers for Cincinnati, Louisville, Natchez, Nashville, St. Louis, &c.

Will always be certain of being taken on without delay, as this Line connects with the Boats at Pittsburgh, carrying the Mail.

OFFICE, N. E. CORNER OF FOURTH AND CHESNUT ST.

For seats apply as above; and at No. 200 Market Street; at the White Swan Hotel, Race Street; at the N. E. corner of Third and Willow Street; No. 31 South Third Street; and at the West Chester House, Broad Street.

A. B. CUMMINGS, Agent.

A line of these keelboats—called Ohio River packets—conducted regular passenger and freight service between Louisville, Cincinnati, and Pittsburgh. On one of these packets you could make a round trip from Cincinnati to Pittsburgh in one month. You lived in a bulletproof cabin with portholes through which you could thrust your gun if it was necessary to disperse a band of marauding Indians. One line advertised that its boat had a one-pounder cannon.

In this atmosphere of bustle and adventure, Nicholas Roosevelt calmly went about his business of introducing the latest thing in transportation. He named his boat *New Orleans* in honor of the destination he hoped to reach. He could not have guessed at the adventures that awaited him.

The *New Orleans* was 116 feet long, with a 20-foot beam. Like the

Clermont it had a slightly rounded hull with the machinery set down in it. It had masts and sails, and was slate blue in color.

Early in the spring of 1811 the ship was tried out on the river and found satisfactory. Finally, on September 26, with Mr. and Mrs. Roosevelt and servants, a pilot and a crew of six, it left Pittsburgh for the long trip down through the heart of the continent.

The country through which the *New Orleans* traveled was vastly different from the wilderness trod by the lonely John Fitch in the 1780's. The population of this land beyond the mountains was now upward of a million and a half. Ohio and Kentucky had been admitted to the Union as states, and Indiana, Michigan, and Illinois had been organized as territories with governors and councils to rule them. All along the river, pioneers were clearing away the forests and building log cabins.

And now, in the fall of 1811, these farmers dropped their plow handles, or their axes, and gaped in disbelief when they saw on the river what looked like a keelboat, except that it had paddle wheels which churned the water and a tall smokestack from which billows of

Louisiana State Museum

black coal smoke rolled. How they must have scratched their heads as the strange craft dwindled in size down the river, leaving only a widening water trail to mark its passage! They did not even know what it was that they had seen. Some of them guessed that it was a traveling sawmill with some kind of machinery aboard to saw logs into planks.

Cincinnati in 1810.

On the second night out the *New Orleans* gave the twenty-six hundred Cincinnatians their first glimpse of a steamboat. Here the boat stopped to take on coal from its own coal mine, bought two years before by the foresighted Roosevelt.

Three days later, on the midnight of October 1, the boat let loose all its stored-up steam as it came into Louisville. The people of the town declared a holiday. They gave the Roosevelts a dinner at which they politely expressed the hope that the boat would not only get down to New Orleans, but also get back *upstream*.

Nicholas Roosevelt gave a return dinner in the cabin of the ship, and while the guests were at the table there was the sound of clanking machinery and hissing steam. The diners rushed out on deck to discover that the *New Orleans* was leaving shore and going upstream! Here was a boat actually going against the current without the help of oars, wind, or a long rope thrown to shore and towed by a crew of men! No doubt many of the diners were relieved when the steamboat returned them safely to shore after an adventurous hour's ride on the river.

Below Louisville were the dangerous falls of the Ohio River, and when the water was high the *New Orleans* left Louisville and ran the rapids to safe water below, missing rocks by inches. Now there was another person aboard—a baby born to Mrs. Roosevelt at Louisville.

Beyond the falls they saw the earth banks of the river crumble and the river surface itself ripple with unaccountable waves. They did not realize it, but these were the first tremors of the Midwest's worst earthquake, the New Madrid earthquake of 1811. Few people today know that the Midwest ever had a bad earthquake, but here was one that ripped long cracks in the earth, caused river islands to disappear, and created such lakes as the big Reelfoot Lake in Tennessee.

Through this earthquake the *New Orleans* steamed on its maiden voyage. At New Madrid, Missouri, they found the town's survivors sitting astraddle logs to escape being swallowed up in the cracks opened by the earthquake. Farther down the river, the *New Orleans* tied up to a tree at the lower end of an island. That night the boat was tossed and jerked about, and in the morning the Roosevelts walked on deck to find that the island had disappeared and their mooring rope was straining down into the water, still attached to a tree that was now deep in the river.

They cut the rope and went on.

Down the Mississippi to Natchez, they were in wilderness broken only by an occasional trading post. With the coal gone from their bunkers, they were forced to stop and cut wood in the forests. At last they reached Natchez, and here again they ran upstream to prove to the citizens that it could be done. At Natchez, too, they made history by taking aboard a load of cotton for New Orleans—the first shipment by steamboat on the Mississippi.

Everywhere along the way they made long stops to talk to people, arrange for trade, and exhibit the boat. It was therefore not until January 12, 1812, that New Orleans got its first glimpse of the craft that had been named for the town. The first trip down the river took three and one-half long months, but it had successfully avoided rocks, snags, and bars on an uncharted river, survived an earthquake, and arrived safely at its destination. Its passage marked the beginning of an epoch in American transportation.

The *New Orleans* was immediately put into service between New Orleans and Natchez, carrying passengers for twenty-five dollars on the upstream trip and eighteen dollars downstream. It was to continue service until in 1814 it became impaled on a stump near Baton Rouge and sank.

We have mentioned that Fulton and Livingston had a monopoly of steam navigation on the Mississippi as they had in several eastern states, but the adventurous men of that day were in no mood to recognize monopolies. Soon after the *New Orleans* made its first trip, other

Mississippi flatboat.

Brown Brothers

Currier and Ives

Traffic on the Mississippi.

men rose to challenge the eastern company's right to the sole use of the river. The second boat on inland waters was the *Comet,* built by Daniel French in 1813. Then came the *Vesuvius,* built by Fulton's company in 1814, and after that the *Enterprise,* constructed in 1814 by French.

The Fulton-Livingston company did not take kindly to these violations of their monopoly, and when the *Enterprise* came into New Orleans they had it seized, even though it happened to be helping the United States win a war by carrying supplies and troops for General Jackson, who was fighting the British forces under General Pakenham in the battle of New Orleans.

One river captain, Henry M. Shreve, fought this monopoly in the courts, and a few years later the company's exclusive right to operate steamboats not only on the Mississippi but in the West was destroyed. Thus, early in the history of steamboats, the waterways of the United States were made open to anyone who cared to build a boat and operate it.

Henry M. Shreve should be remembered because he is the man who developed the most suitable type of steamboat for operation on the Mississippi. He was a man of originality and daring, and in 1815 at Wheeling, on the Ohio River, he had a boat built that suited his own ideas.

The Fulton boats—the *New Orleans* and *Vesuvius*—had rounded hulls which made them draw considerable water. They also had heavy machinery, which drove them still lower in the water.

Shreve decided to build a flatboat hull with two decks on it. Such a boat would skim over the rapids and survive a collision with hidden snags or rocks. To save weight, he decided to use a different type of engine from that used by the Fulton boats. It is important to understand this difference in engines.

Fulton's steam engines were worked not only by the *push* of steam but by the *pull* of a vacuum. Steam, going into the cylinder, pushed the piston down. When this same steam condensed, it formed a vacuum and the vacuum exerted a pull on the piston. Thus the piston was pushed by steam pressure and pulled by vacuum. But that kind of engine required a bulky condenser to reduce the steam to water again.

Shreve did away with the whole vacuum idea. He increased the steam pressure enough so that he did not need a vacuum. This meant that he could eliminate the big condenser and save considerable weight.

He called this new boat—the double-decker with the flatboat hull—the *Washington,* and with it he made a round trip from New Orleans to Louisville in forty-one days, taking twenty-five days on the upward journey and sixteen down. With this remarkable performance, any questions remaining in the minds of the western people disappeared. The steamboat was accepted without reservations. It had proved itself.

Before the introduction of the steamboat, the freight and passenger traffic of the Ohio and the Mississippi valleys was carried on barges of approximately one hundred tons each, and keelboats of about thirty tons each, and innumerable flatboats. The larger boats could make only one trip a year. In fact, the upstream trip, in which the barges had to be poled or hauled by ropes, took more than four months of backbreaking labor.

These barges and keelboats might have satisfied all the demands of the settlements in the West before 1812, but they couldn't have begun

to handle the traffic that was to develop in the next ten years. After the War of 1812, people in the East grew restless. Times were hard and factories and mills were closed down. Poorer families in New England, New York, Virginia, and the Carolinas packed their furniture in wagons and started west. What is now called "The Great Migration" began.

Streams of people poured over the mountains into Ohio, Kentucky, Indiana, Illinois, and across the Mississippi River into Missouri, seeking cheap land and fortune. Along southern trails they came to Alabama and Mississippi, and across the river into Arkansas.

Great caravans containing carpenters, blacksmiths, wheelwrights, masons, and farmers were recruited in the East and went west in a body to clear away the forest, break the sod, and build towns where none had been before.

Cincinnati grew from 2,600 in 1812 to nearly 10,000 in 1820. Louisville swelled from 1,400 to 4,000. All along the Ohio and Mississippi new settlements sprang up. Cabins came into being. Farms and plantations appeared as if by magic.

In the early stages of the great migration, Nicholas Roosevelt and Henry Shreve came forth with their steamboats, providing a swift way of carrying people, lumber, coal, cotton, flour, hides, and salt pork from farm and plantation to city.

Shreve had made the round trip from New Orleans to Louisville in a little over a month. The boats became faster and faster, until the famous *J. M. White* went from New Orleans to St. Louis in three days, twenty-three hours, and nine minutes, and in 1870 the *Robert E. Lee* made the same trip in three days, eighteen hours, and fourteen minutes, an upstream average of about fourteen miles an hour.

Nor were the Ohio and the lower Mississippi the only stretches that invited these new pilots of steam navigation. In 1819, the *Independence* plied up and down the Missouri. On May 10, 1823, Captain Crawford in the *Virginia* ventured up the Mississippi to the Falls of St. Anthony, where the Twin Cities now stand.

In 1829, regular steamboat trade was inaugurated to Fort Leavenworth, Kansas, several hundred miles up the Missouri, and in 1831 the *Yellowstone* got as far as Fort Pierre in what is now South Dakota. Later boats reached Fort Benton in the present state of Montana, in the very foothills of the Rockies. Far in advance of civilization, deep into the country of the Indian and the buffalo, these fire-breathing craft gave warning of the horde of pioneers that was soon to sweep across the continent.

5 · THE FIRST SUPERHIGHWAY

WHILE the Roosevelts were building a steamboat at Pittsburgh, pickaxes were swinging in Maryland on the nation's first great experiment in good roads. The government was building a superhighway from Cumberland, on the Potomac River, to Wheeling on the Ohio, a distance of a hundred and thirty miles across the mountains.

There was no question in anybody's mind about the need for such a road. Ohio had been made a state back in 1803, and the government had agreed to connect the new state with the East by a road. Clearly, Ohioans must have some way of getting their farm goods to market besides rafting them down to New Orleans, then sending them by ocean to Baltimore or New York. Nor did any Ohioans imagine that Roosevelt's steamboat would help much. Imagine yourself a citizen of Pittsburgh, wanting to sell your barreled pork in New York, and having to ship it by way of New Orleans! One can understand how much of a handicap the lack of transportation was to a nation that was growing rapidly.

So the government planned to sell its public lands in Ohio and use 2 per cent of the proceeds to tie the new state to the rest of the nation with a road.

Surprisingly good engineering went into the National Road. Gangs of men cleared a right of way sixty-eight feet wide, down the center of which ran a thirty-foot strip of macadam. For foundation there was about a foot of crushed rock. On top of the rock, gravel was laid for a surface. The road was crowned and ditched to drain off the water, and there was no grade greater than five degrees. Solid stone culverts and bridges carried the road across gullies and streams.

The act creating the highway was passed in 1806 during the administration of President Jefferson; the first contracts were let in 1811;

Coaching through the Catskill Mountains, on the Post Road from New York to Albany.

Black Star

the first stage ran through to Wheeling on August 1, 1817; and the road was officially declared completed, to that point, in 1818.

The cost from Cumberland to Wheeling was about thirteen thousand dollars a mile. (Today, a simple oil-bound macadam road in a rural area costs at least five times as much.) Later the road was extended through Ohio and Indiana to Vandalia, Illinois, where the project was abandoned. The total amount spent by the government on the entire route was close to seven millions.

The National Road was not the first good stone highway in the United States. Back in the 1790's, an Englishman had tried to travel from Philadelphia to Lancaster, a distance of sixty-six miles. The Englishman, thinking of the excellent highways in his own land, must have smiled when he saw how this road was built. It was constructed

Eighteenth-century road construction.

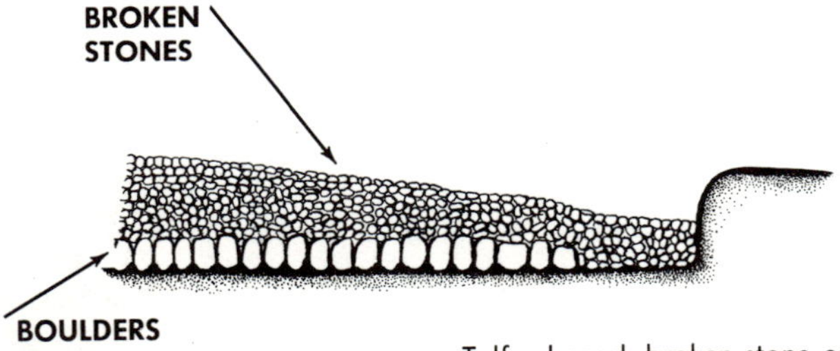

Telford road, broken stone over boulders fitted together for a bottom layer. Thickness of road tapers off toward side.

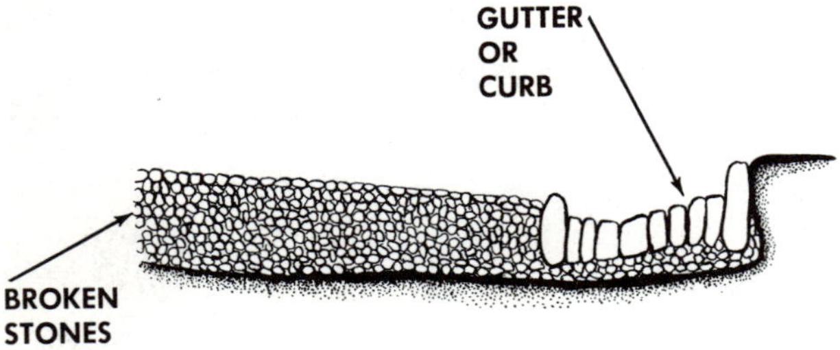

Macadam road. Broken stone of uniform size, with a gutter or curb of large rock at side.

of large boulders with earth packed in between. The first heavy rain washed out the earth, leaving large, irregular stones over which the wheels of the springless stagecoaches jounced and lurched.

"That's not the way to build a road," he told the turnpike company.

"How do you do it, then?" the officials asked him.

So he showed them how a certain Scotsman called McAdam—after whom macadam roads are named—was doing it in the old country. You broke up your boulders into smallish rocks and made your road out of that, then crowned the road slightly to let the rain run off. This kind of road became better packed as wagon wheels rolled over it.

The road from Philadelphia to Lancaster, as rebuilt by the Englishman, was so successful that travelers of the day called it the only good piece of turnpike in the nation. Naturally, when the government decided to build the National Road, it used much the same type of construction as in the Lancaster Turnpike.

The opening of the National Road created a host of new activities. Inns were needed, and blacksmith shops, stage lines and freight wagon lines, thousands of new horses, and drivers.

Rival coach lines developed, most of them with headquarters in Uniontown, Pennsylvania. The National Road Stage, June Bug, Good Intent, and Stockton lines were famous in their day, competing against each other on the basis of speed and comfort, just as do the railroads, bus lines, air lines, and steamship lines of today.

Over the winding turns and grades, the passenger coaches made eight to ten miles an hour. Most of them were drawn by six horses, and it must have been a picturesque sight to watch them approach an inn yard at the gallop and draw up in a cloud of dust, the horses champing on their bits, their coats glistening with sweat.

In the inn yard, the driver would throw the reins to the stablemen who would unhitch the tired horses, put fresh ones in their places, hook them up, and toss the reins to the driver. With a crack of the whip he'd be off for the next relay station, a dozen miles down the road.

Brown Brothers

Concord coach.

The coaches themselves evolved into the Concord type with brilliant decorations and silk upholstery. There were three seats accommodating nine passengers inside, and room for one more passenger beside the driver on the high seat outside. In these comfortable coaches the passengers swayed around curves on the swiftest travel then known, and now and then a coach pitched over a mountainside, carrying to their death the passengers, horses, and driver.

In the inns at night, travelers gathered in the large assembly room with its immense fireplace, to trade news and gossip before going to bed. The next morning, frequently before dawn, they were up again, eating breakfast, urged by the driver to hurry so that the trip could be made on time.

A constant procession of Conestoga wagons carried the increasing freight between Ohio and the East. The Conestoga wagon was the great freight carrier of the day, and it was to serve the needs of emigrants all the way across the vast continent, until the railroads came.

The body of the Conestoga was curved upward at each end so that the contents would not spill out. The underbody was invariably blue, the upper woodwork red, and the canvas top white. One wagon might carry as many as five tons of freight.

The freight traffic was enormous. In the single year of 1822, one Wheeling commission house unloaded 1,081 wagons and paid freight charges of $90,000. Household goods, nails, iron for blacksmith shops, clothing, and tools were some of the supplies that went westward to Wheeling in Conestoga wagons. Grain, salt pork, whiskey, hides, hemp, dried fruits, and other products of a growing farm community went east.

At night these freight drivers stopped at their own inns, called "wagon stands," unhitched their horses, and tied them on each side of the wagon tongue. Along the tongue they fastened a feed trough and there the horses stood all night, in all kinds of weather, while the drivers gathered in the inn to eat, drink, and carouse until finally they rolled up in blankets on the floor of the room and went to sleep.

Imagine yourself to be Ike Jones, a teamster for a freight company on the National Road. You might load your capacious wagon with two tons of merchandise in Baltimore, crack your whip over your team of six horses, and be off to Wheeling. You would charge about $4.00 per hundred pounds, or $80 per ton. In two weeks, by easy stages, you would be in Wheeling. There you would take on farm goods from the commission man—three or more tons of it at $60 a ton—and go cracking and swaying over the mountains, back to Baltimore. You would earn $160 going, and $120 returning, or a gross of $280 on the round trip. Since the round trip took about a month, this would be your month's earnings, less tavern cost, horse

A Conestoga wagon with its six-horse team.

Brown Brothers

Carnegie Museum

Conestoga wagon.

feed, and other expenses. Thus was our east-west trade carried on before the days of the railroad.

But the brilliantly colored stagecoaches and Conestoga wagons were not the only traffic on the road. There were long pack trains of mules—the only form of transportation to the West before the National Road—still carrying whatever small freight could be loaded on the back of an animal. There were emigrant families moving out to new homes in their own wagons. And there were immense flocks of sheep and droves of hogs and cattle being driven afoot to eastern cities. Opening the road was like dynamiting a dam, releasing the pent-up tides of trade and migration that gathered under pressure on either side of the mountain.

In the history of the road there are stories of famous exploits. President Van Buren's message to Congress was carried from Frederick, Maryland, to Wheeling, a distance of 222 miles, in twenty-three and one-half hours, an average of nearly ten miles an hour.

Redding Bunting, a tall, red-faced driver with a deep bass voice, drove 131 miles in twelve hours with President Polk's declaration of war against Mexico. That was an average of nearly eleven miles an hour!

But these exploits were merely incidents in the stirring story of the National Road. Besides speeding up transportation between two important parts of the country, the highway reduced the cost of carrying goods. After the success of the Lancaster Pike, Pennsylvania had encouraged the building of roads by private capital—hard-surfaced roads with tolls charged for their use—and in a few years many such turnpikes were built. Before the opening of the National Road, the cost of carrying one hundred pounds from Philadelphia to Pittsburgh over these toll roads was from seven to ten dollars. In 1823 the rate fell to three dollars, and this must have been due to the fact that the National Road, a free road built by the government, was able to carry goods at a lower price. Competing roads, if they were to keep their business, must lower the price too.

While transportation was faster with the development of the National Road, it was slow by comparison with modern standards. It took about a month to transport freight from Baltimore to central Ohio. The passenger stage from Washington to Wheeling took two days and eleven hours, whereas today the trip over the railroad would take eight hours.

Stage coach.

Union Pacific Railroad

Meanwhile, other parts of the country were speeding up their stage travel. The trip from Boston to Providence, a distance of forty miles, took five hours and cost $3.00. Today it takes an hour. You could go from Boston to New York in forty-one hours, traveling night and day, for $11.00, and this was considered remarkable—and uncomfortable. Today it takes four hours and costs about the same.

However, in spite of this impressive good-roads movement in the first three decades of the new century, most of America was stuck in the mud. From Pittsburgh to Erie, a distance of 126 miles, the road was bottomless. In places trees were felled and laid across the road to form what is known as a corduroy surface. If you were so unfortunate as to be forced to make the trip, you could resign yourself to an average speed of less than three miles an hour, count on being in the coach in daylight and dark for forty-six hours, and be prepared at all times to get out and help push the coach through the mud. Our ancestors who traveled the United States a little over a century ago were hardy people.

Christopher Schultz, one of the great travelers of the day, said facetiously that if you were riding a horse and the mud didn't reach beyond your boot tops, the road could be called good.

One of the most interesting facts about the National Road is that it was built by the government as part of an extensive system of internal improvements that was to include canals and river navigation. In other words, the United States started out to create a government-owned transportation system, and there were no objections from anyone. It seemed like a good idea.

Then came the problem of repairing the National Road and keeping it in shape. And the project became too big and unwieldy for a young federal government still feeling its way along. So Washington decided that it was exceeding its powers by entering upon the transportation business on such a large scale. Around 1830, it turned various sections of the National Road over to the states through which the road went, and the states erected toll gates to collect money for upkeep and further road building.

If James Watt had not developed a steam engine some years before, if the mechanical age had not been getting under way, we might have continued with this good-roads movement, started so well in 1811. Like France, England, and Italy we might have connected our cities with fine stone highways, and when the automobile came along in 1900 there would have been all-weather roads for them to run on.

But even before the National Road was finished to Wheeling, John Stevens, mentioned in the first chapter, was arguing for a railway. Already, in England, strange little locomotives were drawing cars on experimental tracks. Before America could do much highway building, tracks of iron were to reach out in all directions, linking up cities

Broadway, New York. 1831.

Valentine's Manual

with metal bands. We were not to follow Europe's example. Our civilization was to spread across the continent in record time to the tune of steam whistles and pounding drivers.

Before the railroad came, however, canals were to serve the growing country, and the National Road had something to do with the first major canal experiment. The National Road was not yet finished before New York state began to realize that the Wheeling-to-Cumberland road would divert the waiting streams of humanity and freight far to the south. Baltimore, the natural terminus of the road, would benefit.

So Governor DeWitt Clinton and his associates began working actively on New York's pet idea—the idea of a canal to run from the Hudson River to Lake Erie. There was business to be done with the West, and New York intended to have some of it.

The Erie Canal and the Little Falls on the Mohawk River. *Old engraving*

6 · THE ERIE CANAL

THE ERIE Canal was begun by turning over a spadeful of earth at Rome, New York, on July 4, 1817, the year before the National Road was officially opened to Wheeling. It was completed seven years later at a cost of over seven million dollars, a long ditch running from the Hudson River near Albany to Buffalo on Lake Erie. In its 363 miles of length it had to ascend and descend over six hundred feet by means of eighty-three locks, and cross above rivers and valleys on eighteen aqueducts built of cut stone. It was

America's greatest engineering feat up to that time. For a state of a million and a half people, in a countryside largely wilderness, and without help from the federal government or other states, it was a courageous undertaking.

The idea of a canal through upper New York state had been discussed off and on for nearly a century before construction began. Its location was dictated by geography, because only in upper New York did the great barrier of the Allegheny Mountains level off into low-lying, rolling land, and only here did the Mohawk Valley provide a feasible avenue through the eastern part of the state to the Hudson River.

As early as 1786, Christopher Colles, an Irish engineer who had come to the United states ten years before, petitioned the New York state legislature to improve the Mohawk River and perhaps extend inland navigation as far as Lake Erie. About the same time the idea was vigorously advanced by a young man named Elkanah Watson, who carried messages to Benjamin Franklin in Paris during the

Elkanah Watson.
Hudson Historical Bureau

Revolutionary War. The usefulness of Europe's canals impressed him, and when he returned to this country he actively promoted waterways here. Especially did he like the idea of connecting Lake Ontario with the Hudson River by way of the Mohawk, which slanted into the Hudson above Albany. Under Watson's leadership, in 1796 the Mohawk was made navigable by building locks around the rapids.

During Jefferson's second term, the state tried to induce the federal government to help out, but Jefferson, though he was sympathetic to the idea, said that the canal proposal was being advanced a hundred years too soon. Then, without success, New York urged the state of Ohio and the territory of Indiana to co-operate. The War of 1812 delayed matters for a few more years, and finally, after the war, the state decided to undertake the project alone.

Canals were not a new thing in civilized countries. In Europe, canals had been in use for over two hundred years, and the science of lock construction was well known.

Nor were canals new in the United States. Washington had headed companies organized to build short canals around the rapids on the James and the Potomac rivers. The Carondelet, which gave New Orleans a short cut to the Gulf by way of Lake Pontchartrain, had been opened in 1794. The South Hadley Falls Canal, which made the Connecticut River navigable, was opened the same year.

The more ambitious Santee Canal, bringing trade to Charleston, South Carolina, from the middle of the state, was completed in 1800 at a cost of $750,000. The Middlesex, connecting Boston with the granite quarries and timber of New Hampshire, was finished in 1803 and cost $528,000.

DeWitt Clinton was the man around whom the canal enthusiasts rallied. He was born in Little Britain, New York, on March 2, 1769, and was graduated from King's College, now Columbia University, in 1786. He was admitted to the bar, but instead of going into private practice he became secretary to his uncle, George Clinton, then governor of New York.

By taking vigorous part in all the issues of the day he became well known and in 1802 was elected United States Senator. Just a year later he left the Senate to become mayor of New York, a position he held almost continuously until 1815. In 1810 he served on a commission to survey a route for the canal, and in 1815 he was asked to write a memorial on the subject to the state legislature.

When our forefathers wished to promote a project requiring public support they wrote a memorial, a paper setting forth in glowing terms the advantages of the project. Clinton's memorial was so effective that within a year a petition bearing a hundred thousand names was presented to the legislature.

"As a bond of union between the Atlantic and western states," he wrote, "it (the canal) may prevent the dismemberment of the American Empire. As an organ of communication between the Hudson, the Mississippi, the St. Lawrence, and the great lakes of the north and west and their tributary rivers, it will create the greatest inland trade ever witnessed. The most fertile and extensive regions of America will avail themselves of its facilities for a market. All their surplus productions will concentrate in the city of New York . . . And before the revolution of a century, the whole island of Manhattan, covered with habitations and replenished with a dense population, will constitute one vast city."

There was nothing modest about Clinton's dream. Nor, in the light of today, was there much exaggeration in it. But undoubtedly, while he spoke of holding the Union together, he was casting a speculative eye to the south, where the National Road was unrolling westward, toward that same Ohio country with which New York wished to trade. Already wagons were rumbling along that road. Baltimore merchants were making money. Why shouldn't New York have some of that business?

Clinton was elected governor in 1817 and in that year a bill passed the legislature providing revenue to begin operations. The money was to be raised by a tax on salt of twelve and one-half cents a bushel, proceeds from lotteries and duties on auctions, and a one-dollar tax on each steamboat passage on the Hudson of more than one hundred

Canal Boats in the North River, New York.

miles. Thus the boats of Fulton and Livingston were helping to build a new system of travel in the nation. On July 4, a spade was thrust into the ground and work was begun.

To start a great project such as the Erie takes the active promotion of a man like Clinton, a man of magnetic personality and prestige. But it also requires practical men who can meet Nature's obstacles and overcome them. The Erie developed many such men—three of whom were Benjamin Wright, James Geddes, and Canvass White.

These three men were called upon to direct the engineering of the canal. None of them was an engineer, for there were no real civil engineers in America at that time. Yet all three had genuine engineering ability.

Benjamin Wright, born at Wethersfield, Connecticut, in 1770, moved with his family to what is now Rome, New York, in 1789, and there he learned to survey farm lands. He surveyed canal routes under Elkanah Watson when New York wished to connect Lake Ontario with the Hudson River by canal in the 1790's. When the Erie was started, he was given the middle section to construct and later he was made chief engineer of the entire canal.

James Geddes, born on a farm near Carlisle, Pennsylvania, in 1763, moved with his family to Onondaga County in central New York in 1794, and there he became a county judge. He, too, learned to survey. Most lawyers and judges of that day knew how to survey, because many court cases involved disputes over the boundary of property.

Canvass White, born at Whitestown, New York, on September 8, 1790, clerked in a store because he was not strong enough to work on a farm. He served as a lieutenant in the War of 1812. In 1816 he was hired as an engineer on the canal project and in 1817 he was sent to England to study the canals of that country. He came back full of information on canal boats, locks, and construction methods.

These three men—a county judge, a surveyor, and a young army officer—became the engineers of the nation's biggest project. To a considerable extent they were forced to write their own textbooks and develop their own methods.

Previous canals in this country had been built with a wheelbarrow and a shovel. These three and their helpers used the plow and the scraper and the work went much faster.

The canal had to be cut through dense forests. The resourceful Erie engineers developed special machines for pulling down trees and uprooting stumps—machines consisting of drums and cables that had never before been used for such purposes. They designed a plow with a sharp cutting edge to slice through the tangled roots of forest ground.

Cement was needed for the locks—not the quicklime mortar that was used in America in that day, but real hydraulic cement that would set into firm blocks. So Canvass White went looking for the right kind of rock and found at Fayetteville, New York, part of what he needed, the rest near Lockport. Then he developed his own method of making cement.

Here and there, the ground was porous with small roots, and to make the ditch watertight the builders lined it with sand and clay. Where the ditch would hold water, it was not lined at all.

They needed a supply of water to feed the dam. Since the level of Lake Erie is higher than that of the Hudson River, some of the canal could be supplied simply by opening the Lake Erie end. But the canal was lifted over high land by locks, and to supply water to these higher portions the engineers dammed brooks and rivers to form reservoirs.

At the east, where the Mohawk River ran through narrow, steep valleys, the canal was cut into the rock banks, half in the river and half in the bank. Here, foundations had to be laid in the bottom of the river and the outer bank raised high enough to protect the canal in flood time.

All of these problems were solved by a few resourceful men, none of whom could rightly be called an engineer. If the name of Clinton is to be remembered as the promoter of the Erie Canal, then the

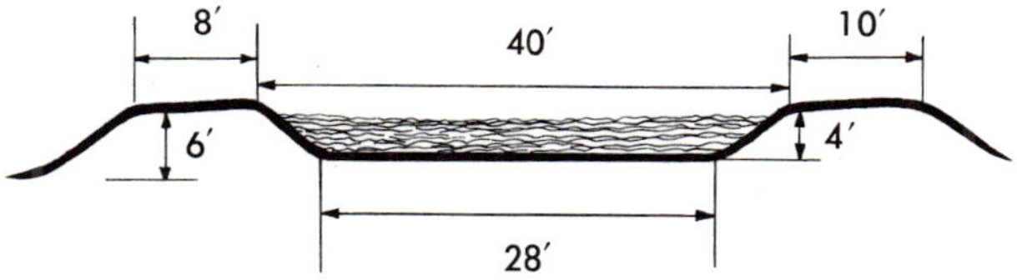

Typical section of the Erie Canal as originally built, four feet deep, twenty-eight feet wide at bottom, forty feet wide at top, banks two feet above normal water level, towpath ten feet wide.

Typical section of the Erie Canal, 1903, after many enlargements, seventy-five feet wide at bottom, twelve feet deep, with stone-lined embankments and a sixteen foot towpath.

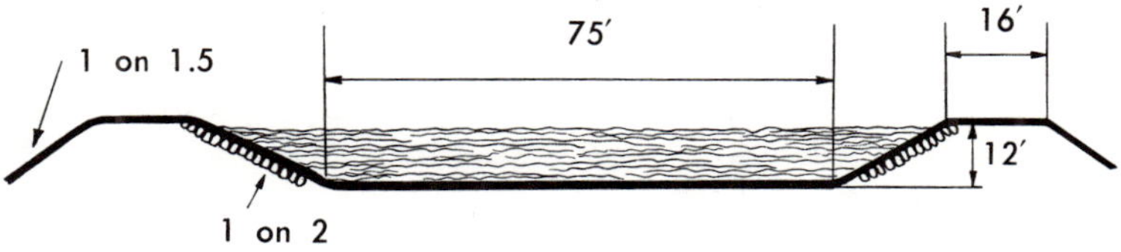

names of Wright, Geddes, and White should be remembered as its builders.

In October, 1819, water was turned into the completed section of the canal between Rome and Utica, and a boat carrying Governor Clinton and his party left Rome to the rejoicing of cannons and bells. By the spring of 1820 a passenger packet came into Syracuse, a small town called into existence by the canal. By 1822 boats were operating over two hundred and twenty miles and tolls were rolling into the city treasury.

In June, 1825, the gates near Buffalo were opened and the waters of Lake Erie were let into the western end of the canal. On October 26, 1825, the final triumphant ceremonies were held.

These ceremonies deserve a short description. There were speeches in Buffalo, after which Governor Clinton and the canal commissioners were escorted to the basin where a line of gaily decorated

Governor Clinton pouring water from Lake Erie into the Hudson River.

Hudson Historical Bureau

canal boats waited—the *Seneca Chief,* the *Superior,* the *Commodore Perry, Buffalo, Lion of the West,* and others.

In the cabin of the *Seneca Chief* were two kegs of Lake Erie water to be poured into the Atlantic Ocean. In another boat, *Noah's Ark,* were symbols of the West, including two Indian boys, a bear, two eagles, and a fawn.

As the procession moved eastward at the pace of a slow walk, cannons, spaced a few miles apart all the way across the state, fired in rapid succession, each firing being the signal for the next cannon in line to blast away. Thus, in eighty minutes, the news traveled to New York City that the first canal boats were in motion. Then, by successive shots going westward, the news came back that New York had heard.

Some days later the procession entered the Hudson and was towed by steamboats down to Sandy Hook, where the water of Lake Erie was poured into the sea, and vials containing water from the Mississippi, Columbia, Thames, Seine, Rhine, Danube, Amazon, La Plata, Orinoco, Ganges, Indus, Gambia, and Nile rivers were also emptied into the Atlantic.

Balls and parties followed. Souvenir medals were struck off and

Design on a ball ticket.

presented to President John Quincy Adams, former Presidents John Adams, Thomas Jefferson, James Madison, and James Monroe, to future President Andrew Jackson, to the Marquis de Lafayette, and other famous men, all of whom had taken a hand in shaping the early history of the nation.

From the very start, the financial success of the canal fulfilled the fondest hopes of Governor Clinton. The tolls in 1825 were $556,000, and in 1826, $765,000; within a few years the receipts not only netted operating costs and interest on the debt, but began to pay off the principal itself.

As early as 1825, 13,110 boats were reported on the Erie and a branch canal that ran north to Lake Champlain. The Erie became a funnel through which freight and humanity poured east and west.

Erie Canal basin at Buffalo.

Towing a canal boat.

Goods that had been rafted down to New Orleans—corn, pork, hams, beeswax, cattle, meal, chickens, fruit, lumber—now began going eastward via the Erie.

The discontented, restless inhabitants of New England drove across Massachusetts to the Hudson River and boarded canal boats for the West. More than half of the New England emigrants, it is estimated, went to their new homes beyond the mountains by the Erie.

Although canal travel was slow—anywhere from a mile and one-half to five miles an hour—it speeded up travel between eastern and western New York. The time from New York City to Buffalo was reduced from twenty days to six. Most important, the canal lowered the cost of freight. By wagon it had cost around $125 a ton to ship goods from Buffalo to New York. By canal the charge was $5.00. Flour from Lake Erie could be delivered to New York for about $1.50 a barrel. Prices like these opened up an entirely new market to the farmers and millers of Ohio, Indiana, and Michigan.

Western New York, which had been a wilderness, rapidly became settled after the opening of the canal. Buffalo, a tiny village before 1825, built 3,400 new houses in that year alone. By 1840 it was a city of 18,213 people. Rochester, Syracuse, and Utica, all on the canal, grew overnight into thriving towns. New York City, the terminal for most of the trade, grew from 152,056 in 1820 to 391,114

Erie Canal at Little Falls.

in 1840. The canal guaranteed New York's position as the first city of the land.

Visualize, for a moment, this new highway of commerce along its serpentine length. It was forty feet wide at the surface of the water and twenty-eight feet wide at the bottom. The depth of water in the channel was only four feet. Along one side ran a ten-foot-wide towpath where a horse or mule walked, pulling the canal boat.

The canal was carried above rivers by aqueducts. The great aqueduct across the Genesee River, 802 feet long, was supported by eleven immense arches of stone set on piers.

Creeks and small rivers passed underneath the canal through big culverts of stone. The canal rose to new levels by locks ninety feet long and fifteen or more feet wide. At the cities it widened into basins which were the boat terminals. It wound through dense forests and pleasant farm lands, and coursed placidly through solid rock.

Water was supplied to the canal from reservoirs, parallel rivers, and lakes. Inspectors walked their beats along the banks, looking for breaks in the walls. In winter the canal was emptied, sandbars dredged out, and new clay lining plastered on where necessary.

The canal itself belonged to the state, but the carriers were owned by private companies who paid tolls to the state for the use of the canal. The builders had thought that the canal would be used only for freight, but people insisted on passenger boats as well, and as a result two kinds of passenger travel sprang up.

For people who had little money there were the line boats, a sort of second-class service. Travel on line boats was unpretentious and cheap, and at a speed of about a mile and one-half an hour. The cost was around a cent and one-half a mile and meals were served for a quarter and up.

The best passenger service was by packet. By putting two horses on a packet and changing them frequently, speeds of five miles an hour were achieved and soon the state was forced to pass speed laws because of the damage to the banks when the packet bumped and gouged into the clay. The very names of the packets—*Flying Cloud, Greyhound, Lightning,* and *Whirlwind*—expressed speed.

Packets were from seventy-five to eighty feet long, eleven feet wide, and not much more than eight feet from water line to roof. The crew was quartered in the bow, and behind the crew's quarters was a small

Erie Canal locks at Lockport.

cabin for ladies. Back of that was a large cabin that served as a lounging room during the day, a restaurant at mealtimes, and the men's cabin at night.

After paying your fare and going aboard, you were assigned a berth number by the captain. You were then free to lounge in the large cabin, or go to the roof where the air was better. If you wished, you could hop off to the towpath and take a walk for exercise.

At mealtime waiters brought sawhorses and planks into the large cabin and set up a table. Some cabins had permanent tables. The food was considered ample and good.

When nighttime came, porters brought in narrow frames of metal or wood with canvas stretched on them. These they affixed to the side of the cabin by rods, suspending them along their outer edge by means of a rope hooked to the ceiling. The men worked until they had both sides of the cabin lined with narrow bunks, three deep. Most packets had twenty-one bunks to the side, or forty-two in the cabin. If there were more than forty-two passengers, the extras were put to bed on the table or the floor.

The mattress was a lumpy straw tick and the pillow a miniature of the mattress. One blanket, usually, was alloted to a passenger. When you went to bed, you were considered finicky if you removed more than your shoes, coat, and hat.

Charles Dickens, on his visit to America, took one look at his berth aboard a packet and called it a bookshelf. Harriet Beecher Stowe, author of *Uncle Tom's Cabin,* said that it was impossibly narrow.

On this shelf you tried to sleep. During the hot days of summer, mosquitoes and bugs made sleep impossible. If you tried to go aloft for air, the captain told you that you might roll off the roof and drown. Or, if you stood up, a low bridge might knock you unconscious.

So you lay cramped in your bunk, hoping that the heavy passenger in the berth above wouldn't break through his canvas bed and fall down on you. As early as possible in the morning you got up, went

Brown Brothers

A packet on the Erie Canal.

outside, dipped muddy water from the canal with a bucket, and washed yourself.

That was packet travel in the 1830's and 1840's, and people didn't mind. It was a great improvement over the impossible clay roads of the day.

In the 1840's you could, if you wished, go from New York to Cincinnati, a distance of 1,100 miles, almost entirely by water. You took a steamboat to Albany, a stage to Schenectady, canal to Buffalo, steamboat to Cleveland, canal to Portsmouth on the Ohio River, and steamboat to Cincinnati. Total fare, $14.75. Time, one month.

Many people did exactly that, but travelers in a hurry took the National Road to Wheeling and steamboat to Cincinnati.

In spite of the competition of railroads and highways, the Erie Canal has been in continuous use since its completion in 1825, and over the years it has been enlarged many times to accommodate larger and larger boats and barges. Today the state's canal system is known as the New York State Barge Canal. The waterway is now 125 feet wide where it goes through soil and somewhat narrower in rock, and the locks are over 300 feet long and 45 feet wide.

What was the United States like in 1825, when the Erie Canal was opened along its entire route? John Quincy Adams, the sixth President, had been inaugurated on March 4. He was taking over the management of a country that was still sleepily agricultural, still having trouble going from place to place.

Except for the textile industry, there was almost no manufactur-

Erie Canal locks.

ing. Textiles had grown from 130,000 spindles in 1815 to almost a million in 1825, mainly in New England.

Iron was discovered in southeast Ohio and Kentucky in 1825, but the great iron mines of northern Michigan and Minnesota were untouched. When the railroads were to get under way a few years later, they would have to buy their iron rails from England. The United States had no iron industry worthy of the name.

Not many people were coming over from Europe. Immigration was at the rate of about eight thousand a year. But that was only the calm before the storm. By 1830, some fifty thousand a year were to come from across the waters, seeking opportunity and independence in a new land, and most of these, finding little chance for happiness in the East, were to go west where they could buy land for a dollar and a quarter an acre; where a man with a hundred dollars could set himself up as lord of his own domain.

Farming itself was almost as primitive as that of the Egyptians. Grain was still sown by hand from a bag, reaped with a sickle, and threshed with a flail. Corn was cultivated with a hoe. The day of farm machinery had not yet arrived.

America was a quiet, primitive country, but the men had already reached maturity who were to bring forth a third method of transportation, a network of iron rails, wooden coaches, and steam locomotives, ushering in the era of power that had been promised back in 1789, when Washington rode north to be inaugurated first President of the United States.

First railroad car in the United States. *Brown Brothers*

7 · RAILROAD BEGINNINGS

THE railroad was not an invention. It was merely a putting-together of ideas already in existence. A railroad, after all, is merely a track on which some kind of mechanical power is used to draw cars. Both tracks and steam power were well-developed inventions before the dawn of the railroad era. They simply had not yet been put together.

Tracks came first. For several hundred years men had used wooden tracks to connect mines and quarries with near-by waterways, and in time they surfaced the wood rails with iron straps to prevent wear. The United States had several such tracks long before it had steam railroads. One of them connected Gridley Bryant's stone quarries at Quincy, Massachusetts, with a wharf on the Neponset River, three miles away. Over this track, horses hauled stone for the building of Bunker Hill Monument.

Thomas Leiper had a similar track near Philadelphia, also serving a stone quarry. A third track connected the anthracite coal mines at Carbondale, Pennsylvania, with a canal terminal at Honesdale, and undoubtedly there were other such tracks around the country. All of them used horse-drawn wagons with flanged or grooved wheels so that the wagons would not run off the rails. They were simply an improvement over the rough highways of the day.

It was inevitable that someone, sooner or later, would think of using steam power instead of horses to draw wagons over the tracks. The use of steam power had been developed by Newcomen and improved by Watt and applied to boats, all before 1800. The next idea was logical. If steam could propel a boat through water, it could drag a wagon on land.

To England goes the credit for putting the idea into practice. In 1801 a Cornishman named Richard Trevithick put a steam engine on wheels and ran it on the highway. In 1804 he built another engine and put it on rails. People at that time thought of it merely as a stunt, but Richard Trevithick had actually, for the first time in history, operated a railway locomotive. For nearly twenty years, England

Trevithick engine.

toyed and experimented with the idea, but from 1821 on, it began to build railroads in earnest.

The United States did not take up this development until seven or eight years later, although it might have beaten England by the same margin if the country had listened to John Stevens of Hoboken, New Jersey. Stevens was born in 1749 and was graduated with a law degree from King's College (Columbia University) in 1768. He served as a colonel in the Revolution and afterwards took up the study of steam engineering. Interested in inventions, he sponsored the Patent Law to protect inventors and saw it passed by Congress in 1790. He built and operated steamboats and started the first steam ferry in the world, a line running from Hoboken to New York.

Stevens was a rare combination of practical man and dreamer, and he proposed a steam railway to the country as early as 1812. In that year when New York was actively promoting the Erie Canal, Stevens suggested that the state build a railroad instead.

"Let a railway of timber be formed between Lake Erie and Albany," he wrote. "The angle of elevation in no part to exceed one degree . . . The carriage wheels of cast-iron, the rims flat with projecting flanges to fit the surface of the railways. The moving power to be a steam engine, nearly similar to the one on board the *Juliana,* a ferry boat plying between this city (New York) and Hoboken."

For 1812, that was a fairly good description of a railroad. It specified tracks, flanged wheels, and steam locomotives. But Stevens was a prophet ahead of his time, and the minds of men, shackled to the past, could not imagine anything so new and strange. It was seventeen years after Stevens' proposal that the United States took railroads seriously.

People do not risk their money to build a railroad because they believe it would be a pleasant idea to have one around. There must be a pressing need for it, a need so great that it seems certain the line can earn money. The first railroad to provide public rides in this country was the Baltimore & Ohio, and it was started for the purpose of competing with the Erie Canal. The merchants of Baltimore had profited greatly from the western trade that came to them over the National Road, but now much of this trade was going the northern route along the Erie Canal, and the Baltimoreans were becoming concerned over their loss.

Baltimore first considered a canal but decided that the task of running a canal through the Alleghenies was too great. Instead, they would build a railroad to the mountains, carry the cars over the divide by means of inclined planes and cables, and meet the Ohio River at Wheeling. There was business to be done with the rapidly growing West, and a railroad would bring that business to Baltimore.

On February 28, 1827, two years after the completion of the Erie Canal, the B. & O. was chartered. In twelve days the citizens of Baltimore and of Frederick, Maryland, subscribed for two millions of stock, and the city of Baltimore subscribed another half million.

The route was surveyed by army engineers, commissions were sent to England to study the young railroads already in operation there, and on July 4, 1828, the company laid its cornerstone, called "The First Stone" (which may still be seen in Baltimore). At this historic ceremony Charles Carroll of Carrollton, then ninety-one years old, the only living signer of the Declaration of Independence, delivered a speech in which he said that the event was second in importance only to the Declaration.

One of the first questions to be decided by the directors of the B. & O. was whether to use horses or steam power on the track. The track to Ellicott's Mills, thirteen miles away, was completed January 1, 1830, and on that day, over these tracks, one horse drew a car containing twenty-four people at a speed of fifteen miles an hour. Later that same day, one horse drew three cars containing eighty people at eight miles an hour.

All that winter, prominent Baltimoreans and members of Congress from near-by Washington rode the thirteen-mile stretch to Ellicott's Mills for the novelty of it, paying nine cents one way. This was the first public use of a railroad in the United States.

In the first thirty days of operation the road took in a thousand dollars a week. Freight service was installed and soon farm produce was coming into Baltimore by horse car.

By that time, however, a steam locomotive had already been operated on a track in this country. The Delaware and Hudson Canal Company—the line built to transport anthracite coal in northeastern Pennsylvania—had bought a seven-ton English locomotive called the *Stourbridge Lion* and had given it an experimental run on August 8, 1829. The *Lion* had proved too heavy for the company's track. Furthermore, its four wheels were rigidly mounted so that they would run only on a straight track or a very gradual curve, which was satisfactory in England's countryside but not for a railroad built in the hills. The *Lion* was a failure in this country; however, it did get people interested.

Stourbridge Lion.

Finally Peter Cooper of New York, who had property interests in Baltimore, offered to build an experimental steam engine for the B. & O. He came down to Baltimore with his engine—a tiny affair with a fourteen-inch stroke. He had made a boiler about the size of the average water-heating boiler in a home, setting it vertically on a small flatcar. He had then connected the boiler and engine and contrived a system of wheels, pulleys, and levers to turn the wheels. The resulting locomotive was so small that he dubbed it the *Tom Thumb*.

But in the summer of 1830 the little *Tom Thumb* made a speed of eighteen miles an hour over the track to Ellicott's Mills, and a performance such as that could not be ignored. On one of its trips came a memorable race with a horse.

The track between Baltimore and Ellicott's Mills was double, and halfway between the towns was the Relay House where fresh horses were put on the cars. At the Relay House the *Tom Thumb* met a horse-drawn coach, and the driver invited Peter Cooper to race him to Baltimore. Cooper accepted.

In the first mile or so, while the *Tom Thumb* was getting up steam, the horse drew ahead. As steam pressure increased, the locomotive passed the horse and chugged down the track, smoke pouring from its stack.

The race that was won by a horse car.

Just as Cooper was congratulating himself that the race was won, the belt which operated the blower flew off its drum, and without the blower to force a draft through the furnace, steam pressure began to drop. Cooper tried to replace the belt while the car was in motion and, in so doing, lacerated his hand. The pressure dropped further, the engine slowed down, and the horse came from behind to win the race.

Nevertheless, the performance of the *Tom Thumb* convinced the B. & O. engineers that steam power was the thing, and in January, 1831, the railroad advertised for locomotives, offering four thousand dollars for the best one and thirty-five hundred for the next best, specifying that the engine must burn coke or coal, must not exceed three and one-half tons in weight, must draw fifteen tons of freight at fifteen miles an hour, the flanges of the wheels to run on the inside of the rails.

Davis's locomotive, the *York*.

The *York,* built by Phineas Davis, a watchmaker from York, Pennsylvania, won the prize. It came within the weight limit, was mounted on a flatcar, and had a vertical boiler in which the fire came up through the hollow center. The *York* drew a hundred and fifty people at fifteen miles an hour. It hauled a train of five cars. Bystanders who saw the train pulling out of Baltimore in the summer of 1831 declared it one of the grandest, most inspiring sights ever to greet the eyes of man.

But Phineas Davis was not the first successful builder of a locomotive in this country. That honor must go to the West Point Foundry of New York City, which built two locomotives for the South Carolina Railroad in the fall of 1830.

The South Carolina road was built to reach the cotton plantations of interior Georgia. Before its construction, the cotton had been floated down the Savannah River to Savannah, Georgia, and the businessmen of Charleston, South Carolina, not many miles to the north, were not getting enough of the trade. If they wished more, they saw that they must provide some means of transportation between the cotton country of the interior and Charleston. So they decided to run a railroad westward across the state to the town of Hamburg on the Savannah River. The line was chartered on January 30, 1828, nearly a year after the chartering of the B. & O., and in the fall of 1829 Horatio Allen, one of the engineers of the Delaware and Hudson, was brought down to superintend the construction of the road. Allen was the man who had bought the *Stourbridge Lion* and piloted it on its first and only run, and he was convinced that steam power was preferable to horses if the right kind of locomotives could be built.

The South Carolina road received its first locomotive, the *Best Friend of Charleston,* in the fall of 1830. In December the engine made thirty miles an hour alone, and pulled four cars containing from forty to fifty passengers at twenty-one miles per hour. In Janu-

The *Best Friend of Charleston.*

Brown Brothers

ary it was put in regular service and operated satisfactorily until June 17, 1831, when the fireman, tired of hearing the hiss of escaping steam, either sat on or tied down the safety valve. When the pressure became too great for the thin walls of metal, the boiler exploded, destroying the engine and breaking the fireman's hip. By this time, however, the line's second engine, the *West Point,* was in operation, and service was continued without halt.

The South Carolina Railroad never indulged in horse-drawn equipment. It was a steam railroad from the beginning, and at the time of the completion of the line to Hamburg, in September, 1833, it was the longest railroad in the world—136 miles.

We can now put together the timetable of those early attempts at railroading. On February 28, 1827, the B. & O. was chartered. Other railroads had been chartered before this, but on none of them was any work of consequence done until after this date. On January 30, 1828, the South Carolina Railroad was chartered. On August 8, 1829, the first steam locomotive, the English-built *Lion,* was operated on the Delaware and Hudson tracks in northeastern Pennsylvania.

In the summer of 1830, the *Tom Thumb* was operated on the

The *South Carolina* Double Ender

Sailing car tried out in 1829.
Brown Brothers

The *Atlantic,* the first steam engine to enter the city of Washington.

B. & O. tracks. It was the first American-built locomotive to be operated in this country, but was little more than an experimental model. Six months later, the South Carolina road operated the first commercially adequate American-built locomotives. And six months after that—the summer of 1831—the B. & O. began using the successful locomotives of Phineas Davis. Both railroads were built with private capital. Both were built to tap a waiting and profitable trade.

During this time, in the populated centers of the country, other railroads were being organized. All of them were short, and all of them were designed to fill an immediate commercial need.

In far-off New Orleans, the Pontchartrain Railroad Company came into legal existence on January 20, 1830. It was built to connect the busy city of New Orleans with Lake Pontchartrain, thereby providing a more rapid connection with the Gulf of Mexico than by the long delta of the Mississippi. Boats could unload their cargoes from Lake Pontchartrain onto the railroad and get them into New Orleans in short order. The tiny connecting road was opened April 23, 1831, and the following year an English locomotive was run on the track.

Kentucky brought into being the Lexington and Ohio Railroad on January 27, 1830, and four years later the road was formally opened between Lexington and Frankfort. The objective of the road was to connect the interior cities with the Ohio River at Louisville.

Conservative New England was also afire with the railroad fever. On June 8, 1830, Boston promoters organized the Boston and Lowell. The following year, the Boston and Providence was chartered, and on the very next day, Bostonians chartered the Boston and Worcester, hoping that some day it would reach Albany where it could profit from the tremendous traffic flowing east and west on the Erie Canal. Between Albany and Schenectady, the Mohawk and Hudson line—later to become part of the New York Central—started laying track in the summer of 1830, and on this track the famous *DeWitt Clinton* had its first trial a year later.

To illustrate the crudities of those early attempts at steam travel, climb into an open coach for that first trip behind the *DeWitt Clin-*

ton. The entire train, consisting of engine, wood-and-water car, three coaches, and several flatcars, was not much longer than a present-day locomotive. The engine was ten to twelve feet long with a horizontal boiler and a high stack in front. It was built by the same company that had provided the South Carolina road with its first two engines—the West Point Foundry. The car behind the engine contained a barrel of water and a stack of wood for fuel.

The three passenger coaches were merely modified stagecoaches with flanged wheels to fit the rails. The flatcars behind were fitted with benches to accommodate overflow passengers who were eager to make history. Each car was coupled to the other by a three-link chain nearly three feet long.

The engine started forward, and, as it took up the slack in the chain couplings, the cars moved with a jerk that threw passengers off their seats toward the rear. When the train was properly lengthened

The *DeWitt Clinton*.

New York Central System

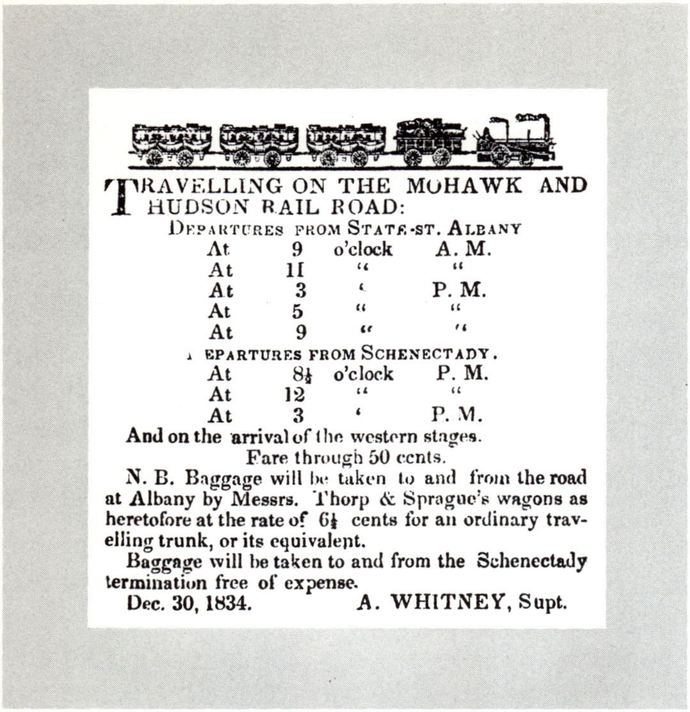

TRAVELLING ON THE MOHAWK AND HUDSON RAIL ROAD:

DEPARTURES FROM STATE-ST. ALBANY

At	9	o'clock	A. M.
At	11	"	"
At	3	"	P. M.
At	5	"	"
At	9	"	"

DEPARTURES FROM SCHENECTADY.

At	8½	o'clock	P. M.
At	12	"	"
At	3	"	P. M.

And on the arrival of the western stages.

Fare through 50 cents.

N. B. Baggage will be taken to and from the road at Albany by Messrs. Thorp & Sprague's wagons as heretofore at the rate of 6¼ cents for an ordinary travelling trunk, or its equivalent.

Baggage will be taken to and from the Schenectady termination free of expense.

Dec. 30, 1834. A. WHITNEY, Supt.

Ticket on the Mohawk.

out it rolled smoothly enough, but as the fire became hotter, sparks and burning embers began showering the unprotected passengers. For a few miles the privileged riders were busy beating out their burning clothes and putting up umbrellas to protect themselves.

When the train stopped to take on water, the cars came together with a series of bumps that piled passengers in the forward ends. To prevent these jolts on the return trip, the riders tore down a rail fence, cut bolts of wood, and wedged them between the cars. When the train went around a slight curve, the bolts on the outside dropped to the ground, and the bolts on the inside were crushed. Travel, in the dawn of the railroad era, was hardly a pleasure jaunt. Pioneer builders were forced to learn their railroading by the trial and error method.

All of these early builders assumed that they were building a sort of toll road on which any person could ride his wagon upon payment of a fee. They planned to have their own equipment and offer a regular schedule of trips, but they saw no reason why private carriages shouldn't also ride the tracks. If two carriages met on the track, one could back up to the nearest sidetrack and let the other by. Railroading, they believed, would be as simple as that. The original concept of railroading was almost as crude as the equipment.

Utica, Schenectada, and Albany,
BY RAIL ROAD.

Trains of Rail-Road Coaches leave as follows:—
(Sunday afternoons omitted.)

On and after Sunday, April 1st. two daily lines, leaving Albany at 8½ o'clock A M., and 7½ P M.

On and after April 10th, three daily lines. viz.

From Albany west,	8½ A. M.	2½ P. M.	7½ night.
Schenectada, west,	9½ "	3½ "	9 "
Utica, east,	9 "	3½ "	9½ "

All baggage must be marked and deposited in the baggage wagon by its owner or person having the charge thereof.

No charge for extra baggage; all baggege positively at the risk of the owner.

Way passengers will attend persenally to the disposition of their baggage at Schenectada

WM C YOUNG,
(52 ly) *Superintendent and Engineer.*

Time table, 1838.

8 · EARLY DAYS OF THE RAILROAD

THE American people had a great deal of fun with the railroad in the six or seven years following 1830. They took turns praising and ridiculing it, while the builders and operators struggled along, running into difficulties and surmounting them.

Train schedules were not very exact. Railroads were merely short lines making connections with stagecoaches and canals, and the train patiently waited until the stagecoach or canal packet arrived, before starting out. And since starting times were so indefinite, nobody knew just when a train would arrive at its destination. There was no telegraph to announce what station a train had reached. Some stations erected high lookouts from which sentries could sight a train several miles down the track, thus giving the stationmaster and passengers a few minutes to get ready for its arrival.

While some early locomotives had wood-block brakes operated by a foot pedal, a few trains had no brakes at all. When a train approached the station, a crew of men ran out, grabbed it wherever a handhold was available, and pulled it to a stop.

Most improvements came about as the result of experience. The maiden trip of the *DeWitt Clinton,* for instance, proved that it would not do to couple cars together with links of chain. A rigid bar was substituted, and finally the coupler and pin, which allowed a little play between cars, but not too much.

The cowcatcher was invented by Isaac Drips of the Camden and Amboy line. After a few cows had been demolished, he decided to install on the front end of the locomotive a little truck bearing two

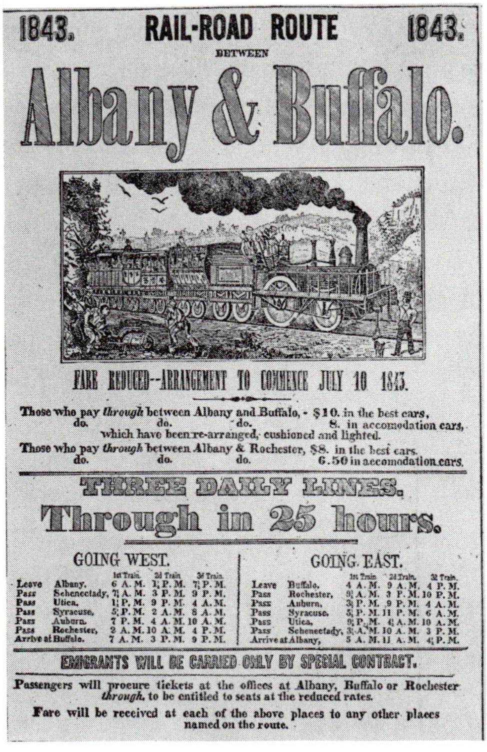

1843. RAIL-ROAD ROUTE 1843.

BETWEEN

Albany & Buffalo.

FARE REDUCED--ARRANGEMENT TO COMMENCE JULY 10 1843.

Those who pay *through* between Albany and Buffalo, - $10. in the best cars,
do. do. do. 8. in accomodation cars, which have been re-arranged, cushioned and lighted.
Those who pay *through* between Albany & Rochester, $8. in the best cars.
do. do. do. 6.50 in accomodation cars.

THREE DAILY LINES.

Through in 25 hours.

GOING WEST.

		1st Train.	2d Train.	3d Train.
Leave	Albany,	6 A. M.	1½ P. M.	7½ P. M.
Pass	Schenectady,	7½ A. M.	3 P. M.	9 P. M.
Pass	Utica,	1½ P. M.	9 P. M.	4 A. M.
Pass	Syracuse,	5½ P. M.	2 A. M.	8 A. M.
Pass	Auburn,	7 P. M.	4 A. M.	10 A. M.
Pass	Rochester,	2 A. M.	10 A. M.	4 P. M.
Arrive at	Buffalo,	7 A. M.	3 P. M.	9 P. M.

GOING EAST.

		1st Train.	2d Train.	3d Train.
Leave	Buffalo,	4 A. M.	9 A. M.	4 P. M.
Pass	Rochester,	9½ A. M.	3 P. M.	10 P. M.
Pass	Auburn,	3½ P. M.	9 P. M.	4 A. M.
Pass	Syracuse,	5½ P. M.	11 P. M.	6 A. M.
Pass	Utica,	9½ P. M.	4½ A. M.	10 A. M.
Pass	Schenectady,	3½ A. M.	10 A. M.	3 P. M.
Arrive at	Albany,	5 A. M.	11 A. M.	4½ P. M.

EMIGRANTS WILL BE CARRIED ONLY BY SPECIAL CONTRACT.

Passengers will procure tickets at the offices at Albany, Buffalo or Rochester *through*, to be entitled to seats at the reduced rates.

Fare will be received at each of the above places to any other places named on the route.

iron bars thrust out like spears, but slanting down toward the track. These bars protected the engine, but sometimes impaled the cows, so he substituted a crosswise bar much like the present-day bumper on an automobile. Eventually the V-shaped cowcatcher came into use.

A plague of grasshoppers that swept Pennsylvania, making the tracks slippery, was the cause of the sandbox. At first, men were detailed to sweep off the tracks, but finally some one conceived the idea of putting boxes of sand on the engine in such a manner that a fine trickle ran continuously onto the track in front of the wheels.

Most early locomotives burned wood, which was carried on a little flatcar behind the engine. If the train ran short of fuel, the crew took axes and went out to the woods and cut more fuel while the passengers waited.

At first there were no headlights because trains did not run at night. The first makeshift headlight is credited both to Pennsylvania and South Carolina, but the probable truth is that a number of roads used it about the same time. A flatcar was put on the train in front of the engine, a layer of sand thrown over the floor, and a bonfire of pine knots built. With a tin reflector behind the bonfire, the track was well lighted for a short distance. This crude arrangement was soon replaced by oil lamps and reflectors.

The tender is loaded with wood. The wide-flaring stack is a spark arrester.

Tracks underwent a swift transformation. The earliest rails were made of wood or stone surfaced with strap iron, the purpose of the strap iron being to protect the wood or stone from wear. In 1830, Colonel Robert L. Stevens, son of John Stevens, sailed to England to buy strap-iron rails for the newly organized Camden and Amboy Railroad. While on the ship he began to wonder if strap iron was the right idea for rails. Why not make the iron rail strong enough to run from one crosstie to the next, instead of being supported along its entire length by wood or stone sills? To pass away his time on the long voyage to England, he whittled his idea of a rail from a piece of wood, and what he whittled was the T-shaped rail that is now in use.

But though the T-shaped rail was invented by a whittling Yankee almost at the start of the railroad era and before long became standard, the gauge—that is, the width of the track—was anything but standard. The South Carolina had a gauge of five feet and the Erie Railroad six feet. The B. & O. used a width of four feet eight and one-half inches. Gauges varied all the way from three feet four inches to six feet, which meant that the engines and cars of one road could not run on the tracks of another road.

This confusion was to last until 1863 when Congress was faced with deciding upon the gauge of the proposed Union Pacific. They made it four feet eight and one-half inches, and eventually all roads rebuilt their tracks to conform to this gauge.

It is interesting to trace the origin of this odd gauge of four feet eight and one-half inches. Before railroads, that was the span of an English cart. When Stephenson began building locomotives in England, he used the same span. Certain American engineers, notably those of the B. & O., adopted the English span. Thus, the uniform railroad gauge of today came from the English cart.

Freight cars, in those early days, were called "burthen" cars, a train of cars was called a "brigade," and the conductor was called the "captain." The passenger cars themselves evolved from the stagecoach. They were hardly more than open wagons with leather curtains to let down in case of rain. One of the first of the B. & O.'s luxury passenger cars was a glorified stagecoach with a capacity of twelve people inside, six passengers on the outside seat at the front, six more at the rear, and twelve on the double sofa on the roof. The passengers on the roof were protected by an awning supported by iron rods.

Just as the automobile, seventy-five years later, broke away from the carriage style into a shape more fitted to its function, so the railroad car soon broke away from the stagecoach style. Before long, the passenger car was a box forty feet long, with an aisle down the middle and seats on each side. A coal stove at one end provided heat in winter. The seats were not upholstered.

Chicago Historical Society

This car was used in 1844 on the Michigan Central Railroad.

One of the first sleeping cars came into use between Baltimore and Philadelphia in 1838. Like the canal packet, three tiers of bunks were set up on either side of the car. As in the packet, these bunks were little more than narrow wooden shelves over which a thin straw mattress was laid. But this car, crude as it was, raised people to a high pitch of enthusiasm. One newspaper writer went so far as to say that you could sleep as comfortably in a train as you could at home, and that the only thing still needed to make train luxury complete was a dining car.

People were even more enthusiastic about the speed of travel on trains. If you lived in Worcester, Massachusetts, in 1830, and wished

The old sleeping cars were not as roomy as this picture makes them look. Wishful thinking on the part of the artist.

to go to Boston on business, you had to spend a day on a stagecoach going the forty-four miles between the two towns. You spent another day transacting your business, and a third day getting home.

But when the railroad opened between the two places in 1835, you could leave Worcester at noon and arrive in Boston three hours later. You could spend an hour transacting business, catch the four o'clock, and be back in Worcester for a late supper. You could do in a day, by train, what had taken three days by stage. Today you can go by airplane from Boston to Chicago, transact business, and be back home the same night, but this is no more marvelous to us than was the Boston-Worcester trip to the people of 1835.

If you were a resident of Washington in the late 1830's, and wished to go to Boston, this is how you did it. You bought a ticket to Baltimore, forty miles away, for $1.60. The tiny engine and cars

Night travel before the days of the sleeper.

whizzed along at an average of sixteen miles per hour, landing you in Baltimore in two and one-half hours.

You waited a half hour in Baltimore, then boarded a train for Philadelphia, ninety-seven miles away. This trip took six hours and cost $3.00. At Philadelphia you had a one and one-half hour wait before getting the New York train. The eighty-eight miles to New York consumed another five hours and cost $4.00.

In New York you stayed overnight and got up early to catch the eight o'clock for Boston. This trip took until six in the evening but cost only $3.00. The entire trip took two days and a night and cost $11.60 in railroad fare. It was slow and inconvenient by present-day standards but it was immensely better than spending a week in a bouncing stagecoach or an indefinite length of time on a coastwise sailing vessel.

As bands of iron began connecting towns and trade centers, it was found that the railroad did more than merely take away some of the trade that had formerly gone to stage lines. It actually increased the amount of travel. When the B. & O. was opened to Frederick, Maryland, sixty-one miles from Baltimore, passenger travel increased from twenty per day to a hundred and twenty per day. People who had been unwilling to go from one city to the other by stagecoach were eager to travel by the swift and novel railroad. Homebound people began to go about and get acquainted with folks in other cities.

The new railroad also changed trade habits. Eastern cities had used Pennsylvania anthracite coal before the coming of the railroad, floating the coal to market on rivers and canals. But when the B. & O. was opened to the Ohio River, West Virginia coal began to come east over its lines. Rich deposits of ore and minerals that could not be used because there was no way to transport them from mine to city now were made available to the nation.

Furthermore, railroads were cheaper to operate than stage lines. A B. & O. locomotive of 1834, the *Arabian,* was operated at a cost of $13.25 a day and did the work of a hundred and thirteen horses. With the young railroads of the 1830's proving their economy so convincingly, it is small wonder that the country succumbed to railroad fever.

From 1830 to 1837 the mileage of track increased from 23 to 1,497. In every state, roads were either being chartered or under actual construction. In almost every town of the Union, promoters were selling stock and promising prosperity to the inhabitants. "Just wait until you get your railroad! Then watch the town grow!"

This enthusiasm brought its inevitable troubles, just as an overindulgence in apple pie will result in a stomach-ache. Building and stock selling went ahead too swiftly, and entirely too much money was invested in railroads from which no return could be expected for a long time.

ALBANY AND BUFFALO RAILROAD.

FREIGHT TARIFF

FOR THE WINTER OF 1844-5.

The rates fixed in this bill include the State Tolls upon the Utica & Schenectady Railroad. Upon the roads west of Utica, the State Tolls, when required by law, will be added.

BETWEEN ALBANY AND	Rome.	Canastota.	SYRACUSE.	Jordan.	AUBURN.	Geneva.	Canandaigua.	ROCHESTER.	Batavia.	Attica.	BUFFALO.
1st Class Merchandise, pr. 1,000 lbs.	4 60	4 80	5 40	5 95	6 18	6 95	7 65	8 55	9 55	9 87	10 83
2d do. do. do.	3 05	3 53	4 02	4 50	4 67	5 29	5 87	6 62	7 52	7 77	8 52
Beef, Pork, Pig Iron and Coal, do.	2 53	2 88	3 29	3 65	3 81	4 36	4 79	5 38	6 03	6 26	6 90
Flour, Meal and Salt, per 1,000 lbs.	2 05	2 30	2 55	2 82	3 00	3 40	3 65	4 05	4 55	4 70	5 18
By Passenger Train, do.	5 75	6 70	7 65	8 55	9 00	10 30	11 45	12 90	14 55	15 12	16 70

Special Contracts will be made at any of the above points for Freight to any other place on the line of the Road.

MERCHANDISE GENERALLY WILL BE RATED AS 1st CLASS, BUT THE FOLLOWING ARTICLES WILL BE RATED AS 2nd CLASS, Viz:

Apples in bbls, Bark, Tanners', Fish, salted, Bran and Shorts, in bags or casks, Candles, Cheese, Cottons, Domestic, in bales, Cider, Glass, Window, Grain, Grindstones, Hay, pressed, Hides, Hops, Iron, Lead, Leather, Lime, Nails, Nest Casks, Plaster, Ploughs, Potatoes, Rags, pressed in bales, Salæratus, Steel, Starch, Soap, Sugar, in hhds. and boxes, Stone, Tallow, Tiles, Vinegar.

SPECIFIC RATES.

Wool & Feathers, unpressed, will be charged twice 2d Class rates. | Furniture, by measure, calling 8 cubic feet 100 lbs., as 1st Class rates; Machinery in frame, or not boxed up, extra, at rates not exceeding double 2d Class rates.

Carriages—at owner's risk as to fire and weather—a one-horse carriage or sleigh will be reckoned as 2,000 lbs., and a two or more horse carriage or sleigh as 3,000 lbs. 2d Class rates.

Live Stock, at the owner's risk, as 2d Class rates. | No single article, however small, will be reckoned less than 100 lbs.

Piano Fortes will be reckoned as 1,000 lbs. each. | Bulky articles will be charged higher in proportion.

☞ *Gunpowder, Friction Matches,* and the like combustibles, not taken on any terms.

No Agent of the respective Corporations is authorized to take charge of Bank Notes, or other valuable papers, or to receive them for transportation over these roads on any conditions.

These Corporations will not hold themselves responsible for any merchandise, unless receipted for by an authorized Agent, and the owner must send duplicate receipts ready for signing.

All goods and merchandise will be at the risk of the owners while in the Corporations' store-houses, and no responsibility will be admitted for any loss or injury, except such as may arise by fire from the locomotive engines, or by negligence of the Agents of the Corporations.

Dated December **16th, 1844.**

C. VAN BENTHUYSEN AND CO., PRINTERS, ALBANY.

And while people were overinvesting in railroads, they were also overinvesting in land. The government owned millions of acres of land in the West and was selling it at a minimum of $1.25 an acre. Speculators and syndicates were buying this land at a tremendous rate, tying up money that was needed for regular trade. In addition, many canals were being built, some of which could not possibly be expected to make money.

But the time arrives in any speculative venture when people come to earth and wonder how wise they have been. Here was a triple venture in railroads, land, and canals. The money was going out but it was not coming back. Builders of roads and canals, trying to get money with which to finish their projects, discovered that funds were no longer available. Building stopped and men were thrown out of work. The panic of 1837 resulted, and for several years the construction of our transportation system was forced to wait until the country caught up, and people regained their confidence.

Just what, during this breathing spell of 1837, was this country of ours like? There were twenty-six states now, the farthest west being Louisiana, Arkansas, and Missouri. Michigan had been made a state in January, 1837.

Chicago, little more than a trading post in 1830, was approaching a population of five thousand. New York was marching past a quarter-million. There were forty-four towns of more than eight thousand population in the nation. The total population of the United States had mounted to 15,532,000. East of the Mississippi the country was

"Five Seconds for Refreshments."

An old print

filling out, but west of the river were only trading posts and forts and pioneer settlements to mark the spots where great cities would later grow.

Martin Van Buren, inaugurated President in 1837, was soon to establish the Treasury Department. Down in Florida the Seminole Indian war was brewing. In Virginia, Cyrus Hall McCormick was working on the reaper he had invented in 1831, so that farmers would no longer have to cut their grain with scythes.

The country, taking fright in 1837, stopped to wonder if perhaps it had not been advancing too swiftly. But it was still growing. Its hardy men and women were still moving westward in a steady stream, even faster, now that a panic had closed the shops of the East and had given the restless men and women a reason for moving on.

The country was resting, but it was gathering its energies for its next conquest of distance and time.

9 · STEAMBOATING FILLS A NEED

WHILE the early railroads were getting under way on the eastern seaboard, the Mississippi steamboat was helping the Midwest get settled. The days you read about—of crowded levees, swift packets, showboats, and singing roustabouts—came to their climax in the two decades before the Civil War.

The early boats of Roosevelt and Shreve were followed by others until in 1831 there were 231 steamboats on the Mississippi. By the middle of the century there were a thousand, with a capacity of

Ewing Galloway

The crowded waterfront of New Orleans.

250,000 tons. New Orleans in those days handled twice as much shipping as New York City. Pittsburgh had more tonnage than Boston, Philadelphia, and Charleston combined.

Shipyards along the river resounded to the noise of hammer and saw. Cincinnati alone, in one year, built forty-five steamboats, Louisville and two Indiana ports just across the river thirty-five, Pittsburgh twenty-five. The docks at St. Louis, New Orleans, and other large river ports held a mile or more of tall-stacked boats, loading and unloading passengers and cargo.

To understand the importance of the steamboat in those years, we must consider for a moment what was happening to the Mississippi Valley. The westward migration that began swelling after the War of 1812 became a torrent in the forties and fifties. At the very beginning of the steamboat era, Illinois, Louisiana, and Mississippi had enough people in them to be admitted as states. Missouri followed in 1821, Arkansas in 1836, Iowa in 1846, and Wisconsin in 1848. By 1858 Minnesota was to be admitted to statehood, thus lining the Mississippi River with full-fledged states along both banks.

And these people, building cities and breaking sod in the great valley, needed transportation. Farmers were raising pork and poultry and grain that had to be shipped somewhere to market. The steamboat provided the transportation. Cincinnati became the great packing center of the nation and its barreled meats went east to Pittsburgh and south to New Orleans by steamboat.

Trees were converted into lumber and the lumber went by steamboat and raft to the new cities along the river.

Nails and iron and coal from Pittsburgh and Wheeling were carried by steamboat to the growing cities of the valley. From Ten-

The New Orleans packet loading cotton.

nessee and Arkansas south, increasing tons of cotton were being ginned and baled, and this cotton had to be sent to textile mills in New England, France, and England. It was rolled onto steamboats by sweating Negroes and carried to New Orleans, there to be transshipped to the factories of the world.

No wonder that steamboats were launched as fast as they could be built! No wonder that for two decades the Mississippi was the greatest river of commerce in the world.

The typical steamboat of the golden age followed the lines laid down by Captain Shreve. Someone has described it as a raft with a boiler on it, and this is nearly true. The hull was shallow, so that it wouldn't draw more than five or six feet loaded. It had to be shallow to navigate the river at low water.

On the main deck, closest to the water, were the boilers and engine. Above that was the boiler deck—really the passenger deck—carrying a double row of cabins with an aisle between. The roof of the cabins formed the hurricane deck and on this was a smaller house containing officers' quarters, called the "texas." Forward of the texas was the pilot house, with tall smokestacks rising on either side of it.

Such a boat cost from twenty to forty thousand dollars to build, although there were many floating palaces that cost two hundred thousand dollars, decked out in scrollwork and gilt, oil paintings and cut-glass chandeliers.

Mark Twain, who was himself a Mississippi River pilot before the Civil War, has given us a fascinating picture of a steamboat's departure from New Orleans in the fifties. Most boats, he tells us, left late in the afternoon, at which time there would be two or three miles of boats lined along the wharves.

The hurricane decks, lined with passengers waving good-by to friends below. Late comers, rushing up the stageplanks holding their hats with one hand and dragging a carpetbag with the other. Bales and boxes of last-minute freight, whirling up the plank. Negroes on the wharf and on the boat, stimulated by the excitement, working at fever pitch, yelling and singing.

Culver Pictures, Inc.

Grand salon of a riverboat.

Columns of black smoke pouring from the twin stacks of each departing boat. Bells jangling down the line. Voices yelling: "All dat ain't goin', please to git ashore." Stageplanks drawn in. Paddle wheels turning, spray flying, people yelling, handkerchiefs fluttering, and boats backing into the stream, leaving gaps in the long rank. Steamers straightening upstream, water foaming, and at last the gaudy boats slide past the city, bound for Natchez, Memphis, and points north.

The upper decks were for passengers, the lower decks for freight.

Nowhere on earth has there been such a task of piloting as that required of the Mississippi River helmsman, and this, too, is described by Mark Twain.

The pilot had to know every bend, every point, every bar, and every snag along the thirteen hundred miles between St. Louis and New Orleans. He had to be able to read the surface of the water and tell whether a sandbar or rock reef lay below. He must recognize the contours of the shore at night as well as by day, for in the moonlight the sharp shadows made the shore look different, and on a starlit night the shore was again different.

Going up stream, the pilot always took advantage of still water, rather than run against the full force of the current, and this meant that he must run first along one shore, then the other. He had to know just where to cross over. Furthermore, channels that were safe at high water were not safe at low, so he had to know when he dared use a certain channel.

The worst of it was that he must continually change this immense library of facts, because the river itself was changing from year to year. The Mississippi was constantly tearing at its banks, cutting out new bends, building new points, and depositing new sandbars. Below Cairo, the river winds like a serpent, here and there forming great loops. During Mark Twain's time, in three instances the river actually shortened itself by cutting through these loops, straightening itself out in its course to the sea. Then the pilot had to learn a new channel.

In high water, when the Mississippi overflowed its banks, it was possible for the steamboat to take short cuts by running over what had been dry land. It was not unusual to see a steamboat paddling past the roof of a shanty or through the aisles of a forest. These short cuts were called "chutes" and all pilots had to know when a chute was safe to run.

Now and then a pilot ran a chute when the water was too low and grounded his boat. In that case, he might stay there for months. Steamboats stranded high and dry, miles from the Mississippi, in the middle of somebody's farm, weren't uncommon.

There were two types of snags that pilots dreaded. Trees along the bank at times fell into the water and lay horizontally just below the surface, swaying up and down with the current. These were called "sawyers," and more than one steamboat hull was cracked by just such a snag.

Another type, with its roots fixed in the bottom of the river and

"Wooding up" on the Mississippi.

its blunt branches just under the surface of the water, was called a "planter." It was a snag of this kind that dealt a death blow to the first steamboat on the Mississippi, the *New Orleans*.

Every year snags took their toll from the great steamboat fleet, but even more were lost from boiler explosions and fire. In those days, boilers were not always well built, and frequently the captain, trying to force his boat at too high a speed, built up a steam pressure that was too great for the boiler to stand.

How tragic a boiler explosion could be may be illustrated by the disaster that overtook the riverboat *Pennsylvania* on a hot midsummer day.

The *Pennsylvania* was steaming north not far below Memphis at six o'clock one morning, with a wood barge made fast to its side. Most steamboats before the Civil War burned wood, and all along the river were woodpiles from which the boats refueled. On the upstream voyage a steamboat would meet a wood flat midstream, make fast to it, and refuel at half speed, then cast the flat adrift and let it float back to its base.

The *Pennsylvania* had finished loading the wood and the officer had just ordered full speed ahead, when four of the eight boilers burst, sending skyward the entire front third of the boat. The pilot, feeling himself rising, muffled his face with his coat to protect himself from scalding steam, landed on the after part of the ship, and got to his feet unhurt.

The ship's carpenter, asleep in his bed, was flung into the river, his mattress still beneath him, and paddled to shore. The captain, sitting in the barber's chair in the after part of the ship, found himself hanging over the edge of a precipice, everything in front of him having been torn away.

These were the freakish pranks of the disaster. Scores were flung into the water to drown. Scalding steam accounted for others. Men and women were pinned under timbers, and fire drove away the rescuers, leaving the helpless people to scream until death ended their suffering.

Mark Twain's brother, Henry, was a clerk on the *Pennsylvania* and was thrown into the water some distance from the boat. Thinking himself unhurt, he swam back to help in the rescue work, only to discover that he was badly injured. Later he died.

Fortunately for the *Pennsylvania,* the wood flat was still made fast to the boat, and into this the surviving passengers were herded. Most boats were not so lucky. A boiler explosion in a flimsy, wooden steamboat, with its triple threat of fire, scalding, and drowning, was one of the risks carelessly assumed by passengers during the heyday of Mississippi traffic.

If boiler explosions formed the tragic background of Mississippi steamboating, racing formed the high thrill and excitement.

Steamboat racing developed naturally from the desire on the part of captains of rival boats to reach port first, in order to obtain a load of cargo. Before long, however, the spirit of rivalry turned

The famous race between the *Natchez* and the *Robert E. Lee.*

racing into a sport that attracted the attention of the entire world. Races were announced in advance, and for weeks people discussed the comparative merits of the boats and laid bets on the result. People lined the banks from New Orleans to St. Louis to witness the spectacle of two steamers flying past, sparks streaming from the stacks and paddles churning the water at top speed.

In preparing for a race the captain would take on no more cargo than that required to trim the ship properly. He would load his bins with the best fuel obtainable—dry wood or coal, with pitch pine, oil, or lard to throw on the fire and make it hotter. Few passengers were taken because passengers might rush from one side of the boat to another, thus throwing it off keel. The captain of the *Robert E. Lee,* getting ready to race the *Natchez* in 1870, even removed furniture from the cabins and took doors off hinges to lighten the load.

This race, perhaps the most famous of them all, began at New Orleans on June 20. The course was 1,275 miles, from New Orleans to St. Louis, and the *Lee* won the race in the record time of three days, eighteen hours, and fourteen minutes.

The *Natchez-Lee* race of 1870 was one of the last-act thrills of the Mississippi steamboat drama. During the Civil War, Confederate and Union blockades had prevented free traffic on the river, and

A midnight race, with passengers crowding the decks.

Louisiana State Museum

after the war twin bands of steel, paralleling the river, began to capture the passenger traffic.

Then a few hardheaded businessmen discovered that it was cheaper to push a string of barges with a tug and thus transport a half-dozen steamboat loads at a time. The railroads and the unromantic barges spelled the finish of the twin-stacked, gaudy, two-decked craft that helped build the Mississippi Valley.

Mark Twain, returning to St. Louis in the eighties to taste once more the thrills of his piloting days, found only a half-dozen boats along the St. Louis wharf where once a full mile of boats had been tied. These ghosts of an ancient day had no regular schedule but had to wait until a cargo could be obtained.

He noted a few improvements. An electric headlight replaced the metal baskets filled with blazing pine knots that had once served to illuminate the shore on landing. The government had charted the river with buoys and markers, thus making easier the pilot's job. But the bustling, shouting, rip-roaring days of Mississippi steamboating were gone forever.

10 · GREAT LAKES STORY

An event of historic importance took place one August day in 1818 at the town of Black Rock, New York, a bustling port on the Niagara River, not far from Buffalo. Most of its citizens were down at the shipyards to celebrate the departure of the first steamboat on Lake Erie.

Construction on the Erie Canal had begun the year before, and Black Rock had hoped to be designated as the western terminus. In this dream the town was to be disappointed, but nobody could take from it the honor of building and launching Lake Erie's first steamboat.

The *Walk-in-the-Water,* constructed by shipbuilder Noah Brown, was a handsome side-wheeler 135 feet long, with two tall masts carrying sails to be used whenever the wind was favorable. There was no cabin deck rising above the gunwales, but in the hull were cabins for one hundred passengers, plus a galley and a dining saloon. On the forward deck a small four-pounder cannon was mounted, not for defense against Indians, but to be fired as the ship approached port, to inform the town of its arrival. It was also to be fired a half-hour before the ship left port, to warn passengers that it was time to come aboard.

Getting the ship under way that memorable August day was something of a problem, because there was a strong current in the Niagara at Black Rock, and the builders weren't at all sure that there was enough power in the engines to move the craft upriver into the still waters of Lake Erie. Just to be certain, they fastened a rope to its side and tied the other end to a team of oxen on shore. With teamsters cracking their whips, the oxen straining into their yokes, and the paddle wheels churning at top speed, the *Walk-in-the-Water* moved slowly but surely against the current, out into the wide waters of the lake. On shore, the onlookers yelled and waved their hats as a deckhand cast off the line and the little ship churned toward the western sky line.

Steamboat travel on the Great Lakes followed ten years after the launching of Fulton's *Clermont* on the Hudson (1807) and six years after the *New Orleans* began its memorable trip down the Ohio and the Mississippi (1811).

In 1817, just a year before the launching of the *Walk-in-the-Water,* two small steamboats had been put into service on Lake Ontario, the Canadian *Frontenac* and the United States ship, the *Ontario.*

Yet it was the *Walk-in-the-Water,* plying the waters of Lake Erie, that is credited with being the first commercially successful steamship on the Great Lakes. From the very start, it earned handsome profits carrying people and freight between Buffalo and Detroit, stopping at all the ports in between.

In those days there was hardly a breakwater or a wharf at any lake port. When the *Walk-in-the-Water* approached Cleveland or the year-old village of Sandusky, it shot off its cannon a mile from shore, then steamed in closer and dropped anchor, whereupon small boats put out from shore loaded with passengers and cargo. If there was a storm, the ship simply rode at anchor, until it was safe to transfer passengers.

All this was crude and inconvenient by present-day standards, yet travelers in the 1820's considered steamboating a great advance over the stagecoach. You could go from Buffalo to Detroit in forty-four hours, instead of spending the better part of a week in a bumpy coach. You could eat in comparative luxury, sleep in a cabin, and enjoy the lake breezes.

The ship's life was short. On November 1, 1821, a little over three years after its launching, the *Walk-in-the-Water* left Black Rock at four in the afternoon and immediately ran into bad weather in Lake Erie. The captain anchored near shore, but hurricane winds tore the ship loose and drove it onto the sandy shallows. Lines were passed from ship to shore and all passengers rescued by means of a skiff pulled along the line.

In its brief life, the *Walk-in-the-Water* had proved that there was much business to be done between the growing ports of the Great Lakes, and the shipowners lost no time in putting a successor, the *Superior,* into service.

The Great Lakes were an ancient and well-known waterway to the white man when the age of steam arrived on Lake Erie. This great system of five fresh-water lakes, joined to the Atlantic by the St. Lawrence River, was the avenue by which French fur traders and missionaries had explored the interior of our continents. For two centuries, the birch-bark canoe had been the craft of commerce on the Great Lakes. In these frail carriers the early French and British explorers had supplied the Indians with beads, trinkets, cloth, guns,

Fur traders risking ambush.

and bullets in return for pelts of beaver, mink, otter, fisher, and marten.

The standard freight canoe used by such explorers and traders as La Salle, Marquette, and Hennepin was an outsize craft measuring thirty-five feet long by five or six feet wide. Into it went sixty packages of furs weighing ninety pounds each, plus eight paddlers, the trader, and one or two companions. Thus loaded, the canoes made unbelievably long journeys through the upper Great Lakes, by portage over into the Ottawa River, and down the Ottawa to Montreal. They traveled close to shore, ready to take shelter at the least sign of a blow. If a rock tore a hole in the canoe, repairs were made with pieces of bark and the pitch from pine trees.

To augment the canoe fleet, the French developed the bateau, a narrow, flat-bottomed craft with a high, projecting bow. It was heavier and sturdier than the canoe, and better able to withstand rough water. They also developed the Mackinaw boat, a clumsy freight barge that had to be towed by bateaux.

The mariners of the Great Lakes were to learn very early that the storms on these fresh-water seas were as violent and treacherous as any on the oceans. The first man to discover this grim fact was René Robert Cavelier de la Salle, who built the first sailing vessel ever to appear on the Lakes. This venture was part of a great dream to establish trading posts and forts throughout the interior of the continent and claim all the land for France.

He built his small schooner above Niagara Falls on what is now the Canadian side of Lake Erie, so that he could sail the length of lakes Erie, Huron, and Michigan without encountering any rapids to block his way.

The *Griffon* was a small two-masted craft of sixty tons, with a high bow and stern. On the forward deck were three twelve-pound cannon and two primitive guns known as arquebuses. The *Griffon* was completed early in the summer of 1679, and with a crew of thirty-four men immediately set out on its first and only voyage of trade and conquest.

La Salle had explored these lakes by canoe and knew the route well. He must have thought, as he sailed the length of Lake Erie and made his slow way up the narrower waters into Lake Huron, how much safer was his stout-timbered ship than those frail birch-bark craft that twisted and buckled with the slightest wave. His eyes must have gleamed as he thought of the rich cargoes of furs the *Griffon* would bring for the great ladies of Paris. But he didn't count on the violence of fresh-water storms.

The *Griffon* paid its respects to the fort on Mackinac Island and continued through the straits into Lake Michigan. It sailed southwestward across Lake Michigan into the harbor of what is now Green Bay, Wisconsin.

Green Bay was the eastern terminus of a long portage via rivers and lakes across Wisconsin into the Mississippi River, and it was a gathering place for Indians and traders. There La Salle loaded the *Griffon* with ten tons of furs and sent it on its way back to Lake Ontario, while he stayed in the Wisconsin country to trade and explore.

Artist's conception

The Griffon.

The *Griffon* was never heard of again. There was a storm the day after it sailed that swallowed up the tiny ship and all its crew, and nobody has ever found a bolt or timber to mark its deathbed.

Men have learned to respect Great Lakes storms since La Salle's day. The periods of violence are many, and they mostly occur in November, when ice and cold add to the terror of the wind. November

25, 1905; November 9, 1913; November 11, 1940—these are days that live in the memory of lake-faring men.

In many ways, storms on the lakes are more dangerous than those on the open seas. In the ocean, a ship may run before a storm. In the landlocked lakes, a ship runs so far, then encounters shore, and if it cannot face the storm it is pounded to pieces. Maritime records state that since the loss of *Griffon* the Great Lakes have claimed over seven thousand ships. The Spanish Main is rightly renowned as the treasure hunter's paradise, but at the bottom of the Great Lakes are strewn gold and silver bullion, copper and zinc, as well as locomotives, automobiles, black coal, and yellow grain.

Sailing vessels dominated the traffic of the Great Lakes up to the successful career of the *Walk-in-the-Water* and for some years thereafter. In 1825, all cargo and passengers on the Great Lakes were transported by some forty sailing ships and two steamers. This small fleet carried lumber, shingles, corn, fish, furs, and whiskey eastward and returned west with passengers, household goods, machinery, and provisions for the growing settlements of the Ohio, Michigan, and Illinois country.

After 1825, the steamboat fleet increased rapidly. By 1833 there were eleven steamboats on the lower lakes, and you could go from Chicago to Buffalo on regular schedules, and continue to New York City by the Erie Canal and the Hudson River, floating on water all the way.

In 1839, Great Lakes traffic passed a milestone with the launching of the *Great Western,* the first inland steamer to boast a cabin deck. All previous ships had housed their passengers inside the hull. The *Great Western* was a magnificent craft, gaudily decorated, famous for the bountiful prairie-chicken dinners served in its ornate dining saloon.

Five years later, the *Empire* made its bow, the first ship of over one thousand tons, and by now a golden flood of grain was riding eastward from Wisconsin, Illinois, Michigan, Indiana, and Ohio, along with barrels of salt pork and bacon. Westward, a swelling torrent of

The Great Western.

settlers, household goods, and machinery poured out, to tame the western frontiers.

All this time, only Lake Superior failed to share in the growing traffic. This was partly because her shores were still a wilderness of spruce and poplar. But it was also because the rapids of the St. Mary's River, dropping eighteen feet from the level of Lake Superior to that of Lake Huron, effectively barred the way to large vessels. There were a canal and a lock around the rapids even then, but the lock was only thirty-five feet long and nine feet wide, just big enough to accommodate a freight canoe.

Then, in 1841, something happened to force the pace of traffic on Lake Superior. A great wealth of copper was reported in the rock hills of the Keweenaw Peninsula of Michigan.

If you look at a map, you will see a long finger of land thrusting northward from Michigan's Upper Peninsula into Lake Superior. Here Dr. Douglass Houghton, Michigan's state geologist, discovered seams of raw, native copper, and within two years hundreds of miners were exploring the region and staking claims.

To add to the excitement, in 1844 large deposits of iron ore were found in the ranges below the Keweenaw Peninsula. Here were the raw materials of an industrial civilization, waiting to be taken as soon as ships could be found to carry them.

Getting the ships into Lake Superior was no simple matter. They had to be dragged overland on rollers by oxen, and in the winter they were hauled up onto skids and pulled over the snow. In this manner, several schooners and two steamships, the propeller ship *Independence* and the side-wheeler *Julia Palmer,* were hauled past the rapids into Lake Superior. These ships, and the few schooners already on the lake, demanded a canal around the rapids of the St. Mary's.

In 1852, after some years of effort, Senators Lewis Cass and Alpheus Felch induced Congress to pass an act granting Michigan 750,000 acres of federal land, to be used as an award to any company building the canal and lock.

The man most responsible for realizing the dream of a canal was Charles T. Harvey, a salesman for the Fairbanks Scale Company of St. Johnsbury, Vermont. Harvey had come north to the village of Sault Ste. Marie, Michigan, to recover from an attack of typhoid fever, and while there he had gathered reports on the mineral resources of the country for his employers, who had invested money in some of the mines of the Upper Peninsula.

Living at the Sault, Harvey saw at first hand the importance of a canal around the rapids. With the permission of his company, he hired an engineer to survey the land, steered his project through the Michigan legislature, and won the contract for his employers. He did more than that—he stayed on the job and supervised the work, surmounting unbelievable obstacles in the course of construction.

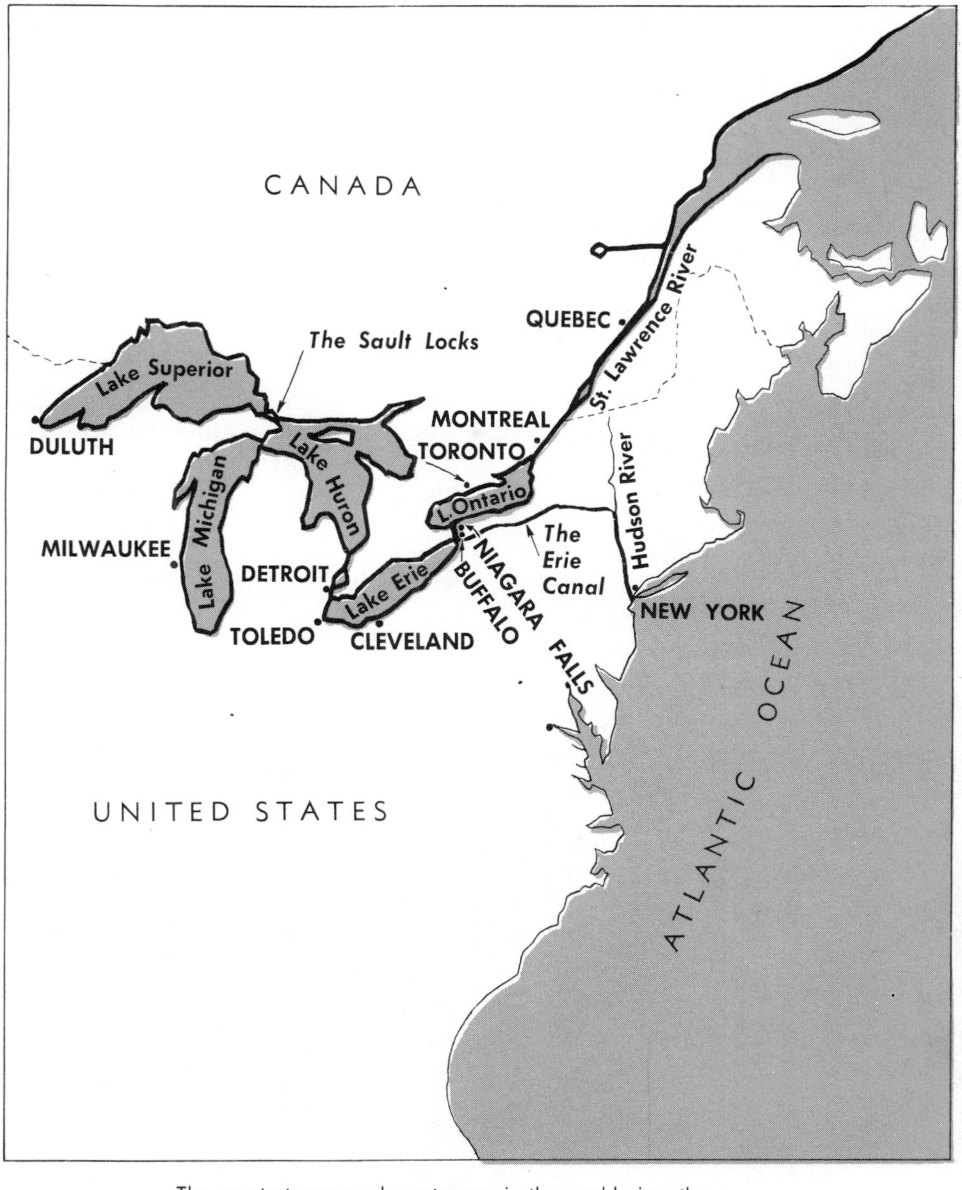

The greatest man-made waterway in the world gives the midwest an access to the ocean.

Consider the difficulties of undertaking a major engineering job at Sault Ste. Marie in the 1850's. The village was isolated in a northern wilderness. No highways, no railroads connected it with civilization. There was no telegraph to speed communication. From December to April, ice would prevent even ships from reaching the Sault.

With a force of four hundred men recruited from the cities to the south and east, many of them immigrants hired off the ships at New York City, Harvey broke ground for the canal on June 4, 1853. He had to build shanties for the labor force, staff a mess hall, build a hospital, and hire doctors. He had to wait out periods of bitter cold that sometimes plunged to minus thirty degrees. Because the town had no machine shops he had to improvise his own methods of repairing

Sault Canal.

machinery and sometimes even invent special tools for special jobs.

In spite of all these handicaps, Harvey completed the canal in May, 1855, within the time limit originally set. This first Sault canal was 5,400 feet long. Two locks in tandem, each 350 feet long and 70 feet wide, raised and lowered the ships a total of 18 feet. The cost of the entire project was just under a million dollars.

The canal was turned over to the state of Michigan on May 31, 1855. On June 18, the steamer *Illinois* passed through the locks going north to Lake Superior. On the same day, the steamer *Baltimore* passed south into Lake Huron. That was the beginning of a traffic that grew to a volume of over a hundred million tons of freight per year.

Today there are four American canals and one Canadian at the Sault. The Davis and Sabin locks are 1,350 feet long—the longest locks in the world. The MacArthur and Poe locks are 800 feet long. From the time the ice breaks up early in April until the St. Mary's River freezes in December, a constant procession of great ships passes through this narrow bottleneck, and upon this parade depends the economic health of a continent.

There is no better place from which to view the traffic of the lakes than at Sault Ste. Marie. The ships you see there are unlike any other ships in the world. Because of the importance of iron ore, special ships were designed to carry it. The ore carrier has a small bridge in the very front of the bow and a small cabin at the stern. In between there is nothing but an expanse of deck along which a series of hatches gives access to the hold. The first such ship was the *R. J. Hackett,* built in 1869, just 211 feet long.

Today's bulk-ore freighters are over 600 feet long, and in 1958 the greatest of them all, the *Edmund Fitzgerald,* 729 feet long, was launched. These latter-day monsters carry up to twenty thousand tons of ore. They are loaded at special docks at Duluth, Minnesota, and Superior, Wisconsin, where ore cars riding a track high in the sky dump their loads into huge hoppers from which the red rust flows into the hatches of the ships. At their destination, the freighters are

Ewing Galloway

Locks linking Lake Superior with Lake Michigan.

emptied by means of huge clamshell buckets called Hulett unloaders, which drop into the hold and bring up tons of ore at a bite.

The United States and Canada are fortunate to have a system of inland seas as vast as the Great Lakes. From the farthest west extremity of Lake Superior in Minnesota to the eastern tip of Lake Ontario in New York state, the distance is about 850 miles. From Fort William on the north shore of Lake Superior to Chicago at the southern end of Lake Michigan, the distance is over 500 miles.

Eight states border these lakes, and in these states are rich deposits of the three principal materials of the steel industry—iron ore, limestone, and coal. It is no accident that our steel industry is located within easy reach of the Great Lakes.

Over this system of waterways flow more than 200,000,000 tons of freight per year. Nearly half of this tonnage is iron ore which is shipped from the iron ranges of Minnesota and Michigan to the hungry blast furnaces of Chicago, Gary, Detroit, Cleveland, Buffalo, and Pittsburgh. Over a quarter of the tonnage is coal which flows from the mines of West Virginia, Indiana, and Illinois to these same furnaces and the cities' coal yards. Millions of tons of wheat course from Duluth and Superior to all the busy ports of the lakes. Automobiles, refrigerators, and all manner of manufactured goods take advantage of low-cost water rates to travel from factory to market.

Two-thirds of this immense and vital traffic moves through a single bottleneck—the locks at Sault Ste. Marie. If some accident were to

Looking upstream at the St. Lawrence Power and Seaway Projects at Sault Sainte Marie.

Power Authority of the State of New York

close these locks, most of our steel mills would have to bank their fires and American industry would slow down to half speed. The Sault locks are a measure of the importance of the Great Lakes to industrial America.

In 1534, almost a century before the landing at Plymouth Rock, the French explorer Jacques Cartier entered the St. Lawrence River, and the men who followed him explored the river until they reached the lakes. They were looking for a short route to the riches of India and they discovered the wealth of America instead.

In 1959, this same river, the St. Lawrence, became a full-fledged seaway, capable of delivering large ocean-going vessels all the way from the Atlantic to the farthest port on Lake Superior.

Although most of the construction on the St. Lawrence Seaway took place in less than five years, between 1954 and 1959, the great dream of a deep-water channel from ocean to lakes has a history of two and one-half centuries. The principal obstacle to navigation on the St. Lawrence is a section about 180 miles long, between Lake Ontario and Montreal. In this stretch of river are rapids through which the river tumbles about 230 feet, with most of the drop occurring in the last 120 miles to Montreal. Early in the 1700's, fur traders were building shallow ditches around these rapids, through which they could float their freight canoes in safety, and in 1783 several canals and locks were completed west of Montreal to bypass the rapids between Lake St. Louis and Lake St. Francis. One of these canals was 900 feet long and seven feet wide, containing three locks forty feet long and two and one-half feet deep, just large enough for canoes and flat-bottomed river boats.

As the continent became settled, these tiny canals were deepened, first to five feet, then nine feet, then fourteen feet, to accommodate larger and larger boats, while the locks were increased in size as well.

Another great obstacle to navigation was Niagara Falls, between Lake Erie and Lake Ontario. To lift boats 326 feet around these falls, Canada completed the Welland Canal in 1833. As originally built, it was nine miles long and contained 40 locks capable of han-

Welland Canal.

Old engraving

dling boats with a seven-foot draft. Welland, too, was improved through the years until in 1932 it was enlarged to the present standards of the St. Lawrence Seaway, which call for a 27-foot channel all the way from ocean to lake. The cost to Canada was $133,000,000.

The final taming of the turbulent St. Lawrence in five years is a magnificent story of cooperation between two friendly nations for their mutual benefit. Yet the decision to go ahead was no sudden one. It was, in fact, preceded by nearly sixty years of negotiation and study.

The story of the St. Lawrence Seaway began in 1895 when the two countries formed the International Waterways Commission, with instructions to report on the feasibility of a deep channel from the Great Lakes to the ocean. About fifteen years later, a body called the International Joint Commission was created to study especially the boundary waters between the two countries, or that part of the river from a point near Massena, New York, westward to Lake Ontario. Along here, the river runs between New York state on the south and the province of Ontario on the north.

In the history of the United States, every new means of transportation has been forced to win out over the opposition of those who felt that their interests would be damaged by it. The National Road, from Baltimore to the Ohio River, was opposed by the people of New York early in the nineteenth century because they felt that trade would be diverted to the south. For the same reason, the business interests of Pennsylvania and Maryland opposed the building of the Erie Canal in New York state. Similarly, the canals fought the coming of the railroads.

When the St. Lawrence Seaway studies began, early in the century, the opposition was even greater, because the studies showed that many interests would be threatened if the project succeeded. In the creation of a deep-water channel, a vast amount of low-cost hydroelectric power could be developed in the International Rapids section, where the St. Lawrence raced downhill over rocks for a distance of forty-four miles. By building dams here, the water would not only be deepened for ship channels, but a total of over two million horsepower of electricity could be created.

Eastern seaports opposed the Seaway because they feared the loss of ocean-going transportation. Similarly, railroads anticipated a loss of revenue. Electric-power companies could hardly be expected to relish the competition of hydroelectric power. For these reasons, although the two governments undertook joint studies before 1910, two World Wars were to pass before public opinion could be marshaled behind the venture.

Meanwhile, the United States and Canada were growing in population and industrial capacity at a rate undreamed of by the cheeriest optimist. The basic material of any industrial nation is steel, and, as the reserves of iron ore began to run low in Minnesota, steel companies in the United States invested large sums in the vast, newly discovered fields of Quebec and Labrador. With this development, the St. Lawrence Seaway gained a new importance, since the ore could travel best by water to Midwestern mills.

A second great need of an industrial nation is power. Although a proposal to develop two million horsepower of electricity might have sounded foolish in 1900, in 1950 the addition of that amount would hardly meet the present needs of Ontario and New York. In the face of these facts, it was inevitable the opposition to the Seaway should crumble.

Developments followed fast after 1952. In that year the New York State Power Authority and the Ontario Hydroelectric Power Commission applied to the International Joint Commission for permission to develop power on behalf of both nations in the International Rapids section. The permission was granted, and a license was issued by the Federal Power Commission.

A little over a year later Congress—knowing that Canada fully intended to build deep-water navigation facilities alone if the United States delayed much longer—passed the Wiley-Dondero Public Law No. 358. This law authorized the United States to build locks and canals in the critical International Rapids section.

Opponents of the project made their last vain attempts to halt the combined power and navigation project by court actions. These failed on June 7, 1954, when the United States Supreme Court ruled in favor of the license to the New York State Power Authority to develop power in cooperation with Canada. June 7, 1954, was the memorable date on which the last obstacle to the Seaway was removed. On August 10 of that year, formal sod-turning ceremonies were conducted at Massena, New York, and at Cornwall, Ontario, and actual construction at long last had begun.

There were now four international bodies at work on the St. Lawrence Seaway and Power Project. To develop electricity, there were the New York State Power Authority and the Ontario Hydroelectric Power Commission. To build the navigation facilities, there were the St. Lawrence Seaway Development Corporation, created by the Wiley-Dondero Act, and the St. Lawrence Seaway Authority of Canada.

It is doubtful if ever a billion-dollar construction program was completed in so short a time. Under the chairmanship of Robert

Power Authority of the State of New York
St. Lawrence State Park with Long Sault Dam at the right.

Moses, the New York State Power Authority shortened its timetable from seven years to five, and the Canadian Commission, taking up the challenge, kept pace. At the same time, the United States engineers went to work on the canals and locks that would bypass the power project, and soon the shovels and draglines, tractors and cement mixers were working overtime.

Most of the action took place north of Massena, New York. Here the Long Sault Rapids of the St. Lawrence swirled around Barnhart

Island on their way to the sea. To still these rapids forever, the engineers built a power dam from Barnhart Island to the Canadian shore, 3.300 feet long and 167 feet high, containing thirty-two generators—sixteen Canadian and sixteen United States—capable of producing 1,880,000 kilowatts of power. It is the second largest power dam in the free world, ranking next to Grand Coulee on the Columbia River in the state of Washington.

Farther upstream, at the head of Barnhart Island, the curving Long Sault Dam was built, 2,960 feet long and 132 feet high, blocking the south channel between Barnhart Island and the United States. About twenty-five miles farther upstream, a third dam, the Iroquois, was constructed to control the flow of the river.

These dams formed a lake twenty-eight miles long and up to four and one-half miles wide, at once creating a new recreation area for the people of two nations, and burying under water river towns that had existed for generations.

To make room for the lake, the Canadian government had to move the homes, stores, and belongings of 6,500 people living in eight villages, creating three new towns safely above the water line. They had to relocate 18 cemeteries, build 40 miles of railroad line and 35 miles of highway. On the United States side, which was less densely populated, 225 farm families and 500 cottage owners were bought out or relocated, and 13 miles of highways were moved to higher ground.

While this was going on, army engineers were building the ten-mile Wiley-Dondero ship canal with the Snell Lock at the downstream end and the Eisenhower Lock above. Between them, the two locks would raise ships 90 feet to the level of the big lake behind the power dam.

Elsewhere along the river, swift activity was going on. At Iroquois, twenty-five miles west of Massena, Canada was building another canal and lock.

Near Montreal, Canada was constructing four locks, dredging channels, and throwing new bridges across the river. Far to the west,

Eisenhower Lock.

Power Authority of the State of New York

in the Thousand Islands section, more channels were being dredged to new depths. In all, the Seaway part of the project consisted of seven new locks, all of them 800 feet long, 80 feet wide, and deep enough to float ships of 27-feet draft.

The figures that dramatize such activity are fantastic. In the International Rapids section, at the height of the action, 22,000 men operating 136 shovels and draglines, 311 tractors, and 249 pieces of railroad equipment, were busy digging up 210,000,000 cubic yards of earth and rock, and pouring 6,000,000 cubic yards of concrete. Throughout this busy period, the great St. Lawrence River, which had traveled its wilful way undisturbed for hundreds of centuries, was made to behave in a most docile manner—its river bed exposed, first here, then there, by means of cofferdams that diverted the swift currents away from the swarms of workers.

The development has brought new vacation goals for the car-traveling public. Along the new lake shore are parks, picnic areas, marinas, and bathing beaches. On the lake itself there is boating and fishing—and the fishing is invariably good wherever a dam forms a new lake. On Barnhart Island itself is the big St. Lawrence State Park, a 30,000-acre area with shelters, a sandy beach, bathhouses, a marina, and areas for family camping and picnicking. To reach it, the tourist travels by tunnel under the Eisenhower Lock. At both the United States and Canadian ends of the long power dam are such facilities as lookout platforms, auditoriums, and museums where visitors may see working models of the turbines and generators that are pouring out streams of power for homes and factories.

The cost has been great—nearly half a billion dollars for the Seaway, where Canada has paid the largest part, and $650,000,000 for the power development, shared equally by the two nations. (The power project has been paid for, not with public funds, but by bonds sold to private investors.) In addition, the United States undertook to deepen channels between the upper Great Lakes, at an estimated cost of $150,000,000.

Even before the Seaway was fully completed, an eager traffic took advantage of the new facilities. In the summer of 1958, after the last cofferdam had been blown up, and water allowed to flow into the new Wiley-Dondero ship canal, 3,000 ships passed through the locks, a forecast of the traffic to come. They bore the registry of Great Britain, Germany, Sweden, Norway, the Netherlands, Denmark, France, Italy, and Panama, as well as of the United States and Canada.

With the formal opening of the Seaway in the summer of 1959, the

St. Lawrence Seaway and Power Project took its place as the greatest man-made waterway in the world, greater than the Suez, which cost $84,000,000, and greater than the Panama Canal, which cost $402,000,000.

Queen Elizabeth and President Eisenhower officially open the St. Lawrence Seaway on June 26, 1959, at Lachine.

Capital Press, Ottawa

The price of the St. Lawrence Seaway was over a billion dollars, but now the ships of the world were finding easy access to the heart of the North American continent; the giant coal, ore, and grain carriers were traveling freely the entire 2,300 miles from Duluth to the sea, from 603 feet altitude to sea level—and where most of the strenuous work took place, scores of industries, many communities, and thousands of homes were being activated and illuminated by power from the Robert Moses–Robert H. Saunders Power Dam.

The St. Lawrence Seaway and Power Project is living and fruitful proof of the human benefits to be gained from friendship and cooperation between nations.

II · THE IRON NETWORK GROWS

In 1840 the United States had just 2,818 miles of railroad, most of it along the eastern seaboard. The traveler could go from near Portsmouth, New Hampshire, with occasional short stage journeys, all the way to Wilmington, North Carolina, by steam. From Charleston, South Carolina, a railroad ran inland almost to Atlanta, Georgia. Another line ran from Savannah nearly to Macon.

Up in New York, steel rails were reaching westward from the Hudson more than halfway across the state. In Pennsylvania, engineers were grading roadbeds into the Allegheny Mountains. The new state of Michigan was ambitiously throwing iron rails westward toward

Lake Michigan, and Ohio was building its first line southward from Lake Erie. Kentucky, Indiana, and Illinois each had a short line.

On these pioneer roads passengers traveled at twelve to twenty miles an hour in cars resembling stagecoaches or rude boxes drawn by dwarf engines.

By 1850 the railroad mileage had reached 9,021. New England, which had never invested very much in canals, was a solid network of lines from the Canadian border to Long Island Sound. In New York State, Albany and Buffalo were connected, and another line, the Erie, was approaching Dunkirk on Lake Erie. Philadelphia and Pittsburgh were almost connected.

In Ohio a line crossed the state from north to south, and in Michigan a railroad ran all the way from Detroit to Lake Michigan.

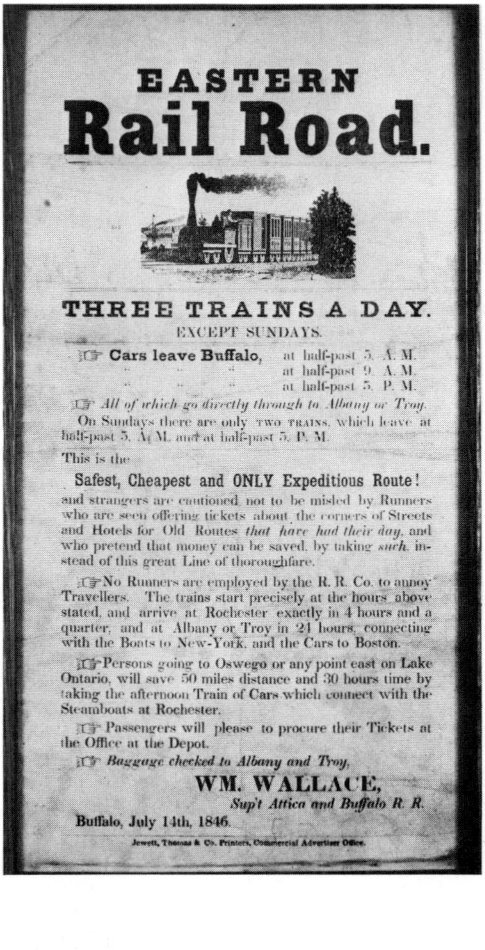

EASTERN

Rail Road.

THREE TRAINS A DAY.

EXCEPT SUNDAYS.

Cars leave Buffalo, at half-past 5. A. M.
" " " at half-past 9. A. M.
" " " at half-past 5. P. M.

All of which go directly through to Albany or Troy.

On Sundays there are only TWO TRAINS, which leave at half-past 5. A. M. and at half-past 5. P. M.

This is the

Safest, Cheapest and ONLY Expeditious Route!

and strangers are cautioned not to be misled by Runners who are seen offering tickets about the corners of Streets and Hotels for Old Routes *that have had their day*, and who pretend that money can be saved, by taking *such*, instead of this great Line of thoroughfare.

No Runners are employed by the R. R. Co. to annoy Travellers. The trains start precisely at the hours above stated, and arrive at Rochester exactly in 4 hours and a quarter, and at Albany or Troy in 24 hours, connecting with the Boats to New-York, and the Cars to Boston.

Persons going to Oswego or any point east on Lake Ontario, will save 50 miles distance and 30 hours time by taking the afternoon Train of Cars which connect with the Steamboats at Rochester.

Passengers will please to procure their Tickets at the Office at the Depot.

Baggage checked to Albany and Troy,

WM. WALLACE,
Sup't Attica and Buffalo R. R.

Buffalo, July 14th, 1846.

Jewett, Thomas & Co. Printers, Commercial Advertiser Office.

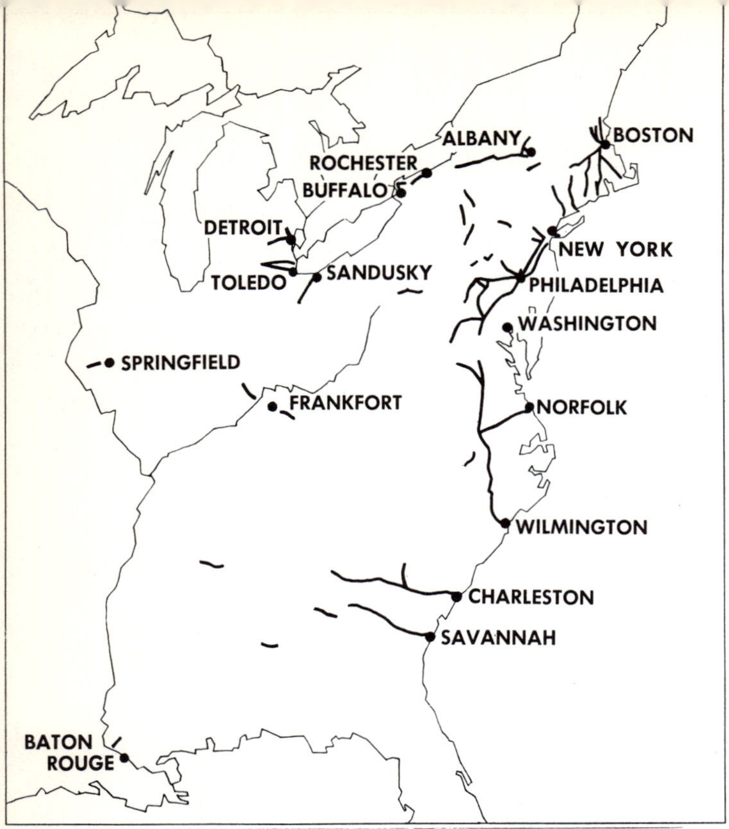

Railroads in 1840.

Bits of disconnected lines, most of them starting at the seaboard or inland waterways, beginning to grow into a pattern.

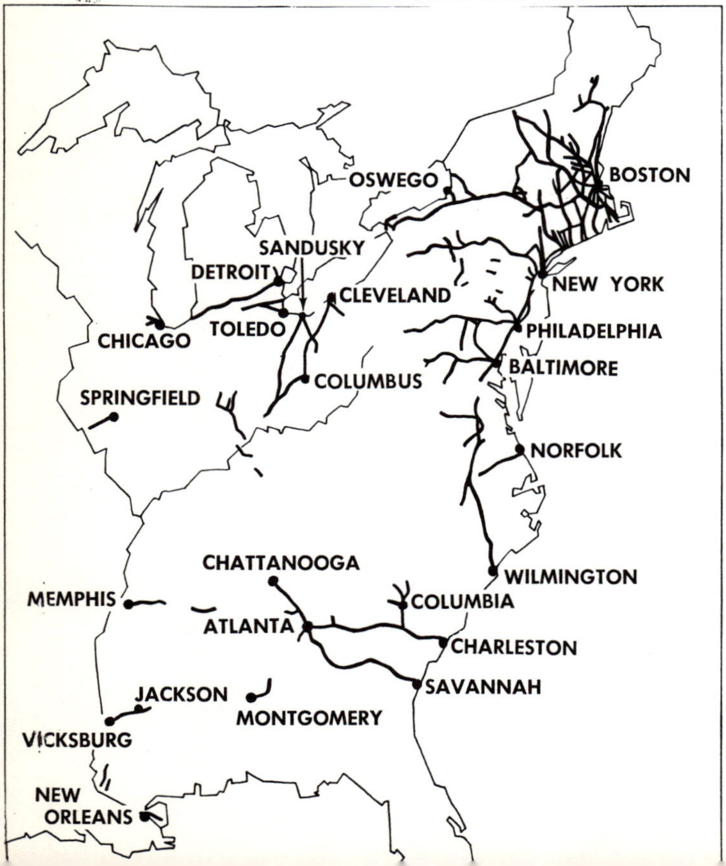

Railroads in 1850.

Beginning to web in the East, longer lines in the West.

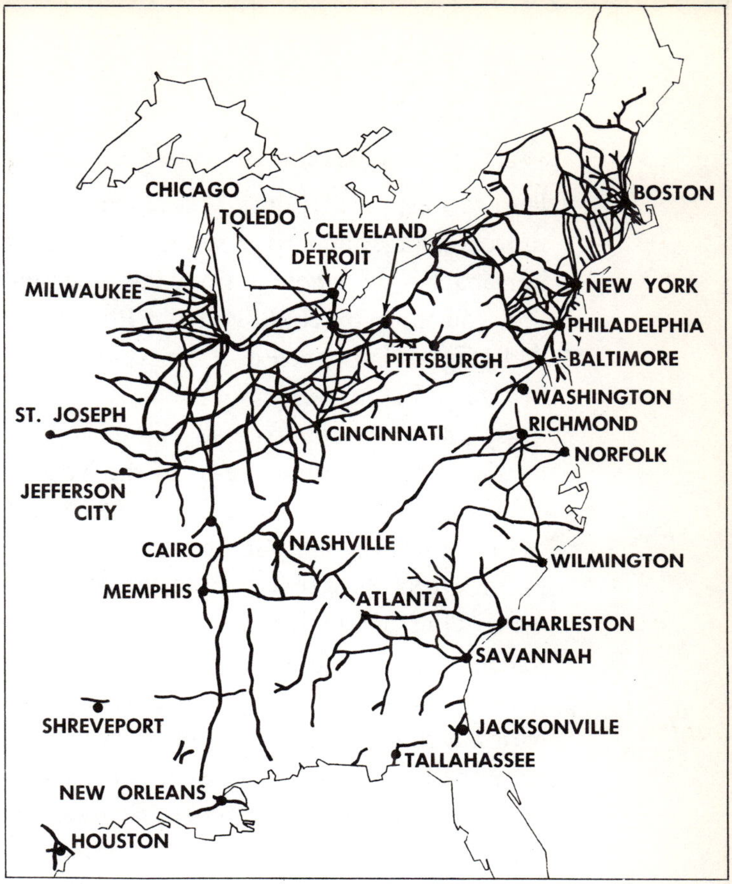

Railroads in 1860.

A thick web in the East, with lines reaching across the Mississippi into Iowa.

Chattanooga, Tennessee, was connected with the Atlantic Ocean both at Charleston, South Carolina, and Savannah, Georgia.

Chicago was building its first line westward toward Galena, Illinois, but still had no through connection with the East. If you wished to go from Chicago to New York, Great Lakes steamers and railroads combined to get you there in six days.

Although nine thousand miles represented progress, the nation's passenger and freight traffic was still mainly conducted by canal, river boat, Great Lakes boat, and coastwise steamer, with the railroads acting as connecting links between waterways. There were a thousand steamboats on the rivers. Canals were thickly webbed in Indiana, Ohio, and the eastern states, and the traffic on them was enormous.

If you were taking a long trip, you invariably used a combination of all forms of travel. If, for instance, you were to go from New England to western Missouri, you reached St. Louis by a combination of railroad, stage, and river steamer, and probably crossed Missouri on horseback—the whole journey taking about two weeks. Travel posters told you that you could go from Philadelphia to New Orleans by rail and stage at an expense of ninety-four dollars in money and a week in time. This in 1850.

By 1860, the country had 30,600 miles of track, and the railroad's conquest of the country east of the Mississippi was nearly complete. You could go by rail from Chicago to New Orleans, and from Bangor, Maine, to Savannah, Georgia. There was a well-established network of lines from the Mississippi to the Atlantic and from the Great Lakes to the Gulf of Mexico. West of the Mississippi, lines were tentatively reaching out into Iowa, Missouri, and Louisiana.

Passengers in those days traveled in gaudily painted wooden coaches with flat roofs. At night the coaches were lighted either by candles or kerosene lamps. Small stoves at either end of the coach provided heat in winter. Platforms were open. Engines were beginning to look modern, with enclosed cabs for the engineers. The introduction of coal in place of wood was beginning to eliminate the bell-shaped smokestack with its spark arrester.

The period from 1840 to 1860 marked the final conquest of rail over canal. While railroad mileage was increasing from 2,818 to 30,600, canal mileage grew only from 3,300 to 3,700. The canal, which could not be used in winter, which frequently broke its banks, or lacked water during seasons of drought, could not compete with the all-year-round swift-moving railroad.

A number of important things happened to the railroad during the twenty years before the Civil War. The earliest tracks had been hastily laid, with short curves and flimsy trestles across the ravines. Strap-iron rails, imperfectly bolted to their wooden sills, frequently worked loose, curled upward, and thrust themselves through the floors of the coaches. As speeds increased, accidents became more and more frequent.

So the roads began improving their tracks. Curves became wider. Stone and iron bridges replaced wooden trestles. Heavy T-rails replaced strap iron. Where inclined planes had hauled cars over mountains by means of cables and stationary engines, tunnels were now driven through the hills.

In 1844 a startling invention was introduced to the world—an invention that was to improve railway operation. Samuel Finley Breese Morse, a portrait painter and inventor, had spent his spare time tinkering with wires and coils and metal keys until he had evolved a device that he called the "telegraph." It could, he said, send messages by a system of dots and dashes. These messages could travel long distances—across a continent—in a fraction of a second.

He petitioned Congress for a grant of money with which to build a telegraph line and finally obtained thirty thousand dollars. Wires were strung from Baltimore to Washington, and in 1844, before an assemblage of statesmen and scientists, he sent these words from Baltimore to the Capital: "What Hath God Wrought?"

Instantly a new vision of quick communication dazzled men's minds. If a New York financier wished to tell a Chicago agent to buy land, instead of allowing a week for the orders to be transmitted by

Samuel F. B. Morse
Hudson Historical Bureau

The first electromagnetic recording telegraph, 1837. The record was in the form of holes punched in the tape.
Hudson Historical Bureau

mail, in an hour he could send mysterious code signals over a copper wire.

Telegraph poles began to make their appearance on the American landscape, and one of the early lines stretched across New York state, roughly following the tracks of the young Erie Railroad.

At that time, on all single-track railroads, it was necessary to have some agreement by which certain trains would wait at sidings for other trains to pass them. On the Erie line, eastbound trains had the right of way and westbound trains took the siding. But if, by any chance, one train was delayed, the other train was compelled to wait in ignorance until the missing train made its appearance.

In 1850, a westbound Erie train took to a siding and waited vainly for the eastbound to pass. It might have waited a long time if Charles Minot, the superintendent, hadn't been aboard. This man used his head. He went to the telegraph office and wired ahead to find out where the missing train was. When he discovered that it had not yet passed Port Jervis, he wired instructions to the Port Jervis station agent to hold the train there when it arrived.

Then the superintendent ordered his own engineer to proceed. The engineer refused. He did not intend to risk a head-on collision. What if the trains met midway between stations? One of them would have to back up to a siding.

The superintendent took matters into his own hands. He climbed into the cab and jerked at the throttle. The engineer, standing on the ground, woke up in time to catch one of the rear cars. The train proceeded from station to station, and at each telegraph office the superintendent wired ahead to discover the location of the delayed eastbound. By using the new invention, he saved himself and his passengers hours of irksome delay. And he wrote a new page in railroad history.

This is the first recorded use of the telegraph for directing railroad traffic. Out of it came the present system of train dispatching. Today, by the use of both telephone and telegraph, the location of every train is known and traffic is intelligently directed over immense networks of lines without confusion. But it all grew out of the initiative of that superintendent, back in 1850, who dared to use the telegraph to hunt for a missing train.

Another important event in the story of railroads took place during this same period, one that had to do not with operating trains, but getting the money with which to build them.

Ever since the beginning of the railroad, men had tried to get aid from the federal government for the building of the roads. The government had refused, with the result that the roads had been built by private corporations with the help of state and city governments.

Out in the Middle West, however, where population was not very dense and there was little wealth, states were having a difficult time building railroads.

Illinois was one of those states. Since 1836, Illinois had been trying to build a railroad through the center of the state, from Cairo at the south to Galena in the north, with a branch running to Chicago. Galena was then one of the most important cities of the state. Three attempts had been made and considerable money spent in grading, but financial troubles had prevented the completion of the road. In 1850 the Illinois Central was little more than a surveyed route.

Illinois badly needed the railroad. There were 850,000 people in the state in 1850, most of them engaged in agriculture. But only those farmers living near the Mississippi or the Illinois rivers, or in the north close to Lake Michigan, could profitably send their crops to market. The farmers who lived in the interior counties had no effective way to move their produce. The highways were bogs of mud. If men needed to move their bulky grains and cattle more than twenty miles, the cost of transportation was so high there was no profit left.

For lack of transportation the state was throttled. There were thirty-five million fertile acres in Illinois, but only three million of them were in the five staple crops—corn, wheat, oats, rye, and potatoes. One-third of the land still belonged to the United States government. Most of the rest was untouched by a plow. The land would remain that way until some good means of transportation opened up the center of the state.

Stephen A. Douglas, United States Senator from Illinois, asked Congress to help the state build the much-needed railroad. He proposed not only a railroad extending down through Illinois, but on to Mobile, and enlisted the support of Southern senators in the project. He asked Congress to turn over public land to the state, the state in turn to give the land to the railroad. The railroad could sell the land, thus raising money to go ahead with construction. Specifically he asked that the Illinois Central be given alternate sections on each side of the right of way, six miles deep.

In return the railroad would give seven per cent of its gross revenues to the state, and transport troops and other property of the United States government free.

It was an unusual proposal, but Douglas argued that everybody would benefit. The government did not need the land and the state needed the railroad. The value of farm lands along the route would rise with the coming of the railroad, and the remaining government land would increase in value. Illinois farm crops would find a way of

Interior of passenger car, 1850. *Union Pacific Railroad*

getting to eastern cities, and the total wealth of the country would increase.

The law was finally passed on September 20, 1850. The Illinois Central received 2,595,133 acres on which it realized, over a period of years, some twenty million dollars. Illinois built the railroad it needed and from the year of its completion, 1855, the future of the state was assured. Towns sprang up, and agriculture and industry prospered.

This was the first land grant to a railroad. The government was to give away between 150,000,000 and 160,000,000 acres of land to railroads during the next twenty-two years, thereby making possible the construction of railroads to the Pacific Coast long before there were enough people in western states to justify a railroad.

Another important event in the history of railroading occurred before 1860. George M. Pullman, who was born in Brocton, New York, in 1831, when the first railroads were getting under way in this country, made six thousand dollars moving buildings in Albion, New York, at the time the Erie Canal was being widened. He took his tidy fortune to Chicago, where the swampy ground on which part of the city was built required more moving and foundation-raising, and his personal fortune increased to twenty thousand dollars.

But his destiny was not to lie in contracting work of this sort. Back in New York State he had ridden in one of the crude sleepers of the day with its canal-packet shelves and lumpy mattresses. By 1858 there was considerable night travel on railroads, and such sleepers as were then in service were anything but satisfactory.

In that year, when Pullman suggested to the Chicago and Alton road that he convert two of their day coaches into sleepers, they told him to see what he could do. The two coaches he received were the typical flat-roofed cars of the day, forty-four feet long.

Into them George Pullman built ten sleeping car sections, two washrooms, and a linen locker. The cars were lighted by candles and there was a stove at either end. There were no carpets on the floor. The lower berths were made up by dropping the back of the seat until it was level with the seat itself. On the bed thus formed were put a mattress and blankets. Sheets were an unnecessary refinement.

The upper berth was a shelf that was held to the top of the car by a catch when not in use. It could be lowered by pulleys to a point midway between the top of the car and the floor. Into this upper berth the blankets could be packed during the day.

The washrooms of these first Pullmans were so small only one person could occupy them at a time. They contained a tin washbasin that was filled from a water tank. The roofs were so low, a tall man bumped his head on the ceiling. One of these first two sleepers was *No. 9,* and, since it was finished before the other, *No. 9* became historic as Pullman's first sleeper.

During the Civil War Pullman was engaged in other business in

Interior of the first Pullman sleeping car, the famous No. 9.

Exterior of the first Pullman sleeping car.

Colorado, but in 1864, back in Chicago, he went to work on a new sleeper—the famous *Pioneer*. This car was fifty-four feet long and ten feet wide, with more headroom than the two older cars. It was finished in handsome woods and luxurious upholstery, with larger washrooms and every comfort, including sheets and towels. The cost was twenty thousand dollars.

Railroad men said the car was too wide to enter station platforms and too high to go under bridges, to which Pullman answered, "Then alter the platforms and bridges to accommodate larger cars."

That was asking a little too much, and Pullman's car might have rusted in the yard had not a historic tragedy occurred on April 14, 1865. The assassination of Abraham Lincoln, which plunged the nation into the chaos of Reconstruction days, also forced the acceptance of the new Pullman car. Lincoln's body was to be transported in state to Springfield, Illinois, and the *Pioneer* was commandeered for the funeral train between Chicago and Springfield. Platforms and bridges, which could not be altered for an oversized sleeping car, could certainly be altered for a martyred President. So the *Pioneer*'s first trip was the solemn one of accompanying the Emancipator to his final resting place.

Later President Grant used the *Pioneer* between Chicago and his home in Galena. The fame of the new coach spread, the Pullman Palace Car Company was organized in 1867, and the company grew into one of America's big industries. For many years, the Pullmans in use on the railroads belonged not to the railroads but to the Pullman Company, which operated them and charged separately for accommodations. The charge for a bed or a chair on a first-class coach is still a separate one, but today the railroads own the vast majority of sleeping cars. In 1947 the railroads acquired the Pullman Company and employed it to staff and operate the sleeping cars.

An important change in the organization of railroads also occurred in the period up to and including the Civil War. Short lines began to unite into end-to-end combinations. Between Albany and Buffalo, for instance, eleven short roads combined to form the New York

Brown Brothers

An old print showing an early sleeping car.

Central, and the resulting road was able to operate more cheaply and offer continuous service.

So the period up to and including the Civil War saw radical changes in railroad construction and operation. The telegraph for railroad operation, the land grant to aid in construction, the Pullman for passenger comfort, end-to-end combinations—these were four of the outstanding developments of the period. By the end of the Civil War the country had solved its transportation problem east of the Mississippi. The important centers of trade were linked by railroads, steamship lines, and canals, and of the three methods of transportation railroads were rapidly becoming the most important. Intercity highways, on the other hand, were almost completely neglected, probably because it was felt the other three methods of travel satisfied all needs. In the eastern half of the United States, the stagecoach was rapidly becoming a museum piece.

A luxury "drawing-room coach" of 1868, in service between Chicago and Cleveland.

But by then many things had been happening to turn the eyes of America westward. For a long time, Americans had been settling in the land now known as Texas but then belonging to Mexico. In 1836 these settlers declared their independence of Mexico and nine years later their territory was annexed to the United States. The annexation of Texas led to war with Mexico, and the war resulted in our acquiring all the land north of the Rio Grande, including California.

Now our rovers from the East could pack their blankets and stoves and plows into wagons, drive overland to the Pacific Ocean, and be sure that they remained in the United States all the way.

While this was happening to the south, our northern boundary was also being fixed. For a long time there had been some doubt about it, but on June 15, 1846, the United States and England mutually agreed that the United States extended as far north as a line running westward into the Pacific just below Victoria Island. And so settlers following the Oregon trail into the Columbia River valley could be equally sure that they were in their own country.

Two years later, gold was discovered on the American River, inland from the tiny port of San Francisco. Soldiers stationed in San Francisco deserted their regiments and sailors left their ships to become miners. Storekeepers shut up their shops, outfitted themselves with camping equipment, and hurried to the discovery. Stories of men getting rich by panning gold from the river trickled eastward, and in 1849 the gold rush was on.

Men came from Boston, New York, Philadelphia, and Baltimore. They came from the South and the Midwest. Whole shiploads from Europe arrived in San Francisco to hunt gold on the American River and its branches. From the Midwest they came by covered wagon, pack train, and horseback. From the eastern seaboard they sailed to the Isthmus of Panama, went overland to Panama City, and shipped aboard other boats for San Francisco. Some even made the long journey around the Horn of South America.

Nobody knows how many people went to California in 1849, but it is estimated that at least thirty-five thousand went by the overland route, and probably as many more by ship. There was gold enough for only the few lucky ones. The rest discovered a fertile, exciting, beautiful country, and many stayed to become merchants, farmers, and laborers. California was admitted to statehood in September, 1850, with a population of almost one hundred thousand.

These events—war with Mexico, gold, and the settlement of boundaries—all occurring in the middle of the last century, turned everyone's eyes westward. The Pacific regions began to fill up, and as the

Dining car, 1880.

population grew, the need for better transportation became greater.

If the gold rush had not occurred in the railroad era, what would have happened? Californians were separated from the Mississippi by the Rockies and a thousand miles of rolling Indian country. They were a month away by water. In time, a highway like the National Road would undoubtedly have been built, but even after it was finished, the Mississippi would have been weeks away.

But the fifties were the years of the railroad fever. East of the Mississippi, wherever a new railroad threw out its shining twin tracks, new towns sprang up, new farms checkered the map, land prices boomed, and factories worked overtime to supply the new communities with lumber, furniture, farm machinery, and everything else that people needed. The railroads were another name for Prosperity.

So, when visionaries suggested a transcontinental railroad, nobody laughed. Why not? Suppose it did cost a lot of money! It would pay for itself. Towns held railroad conventions. Congress considered the matter. The idea of a railroad to the Pacific Coast grew.

Union Pacific Railroad

12 · BUILDING THE UNION PACIFIC

To BRIDGE the gap between the discovery of gold in 1848 and the first transcontinental railroad in 1869, the West went back to the stagecoach era that had flourished in the East a generation before. The West, too, had its bouncing Concord coaches, its cumbersome freight wagons, its inns and relay stations where travelers rested and ate, and where fresh horses replaced tired ones.

Yet the stagecoach era of the West was far different from its ancestor. In the East there had been substantial frame or stone inns. The inns of the West were log cabins and adobe huts. In the East there were stableyards. In the West, pole corrals. In the East there had been roads. In the West, trails.

In the East, now and then, there may have been a masked highwayman to relieve passengers of their purses and baggage. In the West there were hostile Indians who—when they did attack—were after scalps and lives. In the East, you slept in a comfortable inn bedroom. In the West, where the stations were often too far apart, you slept on the ground under the stars, with guards posted.

Regular stage lines sprang up very soon after the discovery of gold. In 1850 a line was established from Independence, Missouri, to Salt Lake City, and the next year was extended to San Francisco. At the same time another line, beginning at Independence, was thrown southwest to Santa Fe, from which town you could somehow get to Southern California if you must. In 1850 Los Angeles was a village of 1,600 people and San Francisco a roaring town of 35,000.

Another forward step was taken in 1858 when John Butterfield's famous Overland Mail began its lively career. Butterfield obtained a contract with the government whereby he was to provide twice-a-week service between San Francisco in the west and St. Louis and Memphis in the east. The government was to pay him $600,000 a year for carrying the mail by stagecoach. His route was to follow a

Butterfield's overland mail coach starting out from Atchison, Kansas.

Overland coach office, Denver, Colorado.

great semicircle from San Francisco to Los Angeles, and then eastward to Fort Smith, Arkansas. At that point a branch line was to go to Memphis. The main line would go on to Tipton, Missouri, where connection would be made with the railroad to St. Louis.

Butterfield constructed a hundred and sixty stations where horses could be changed and meals served. He built repair shops and bridges. He employed seven hundred and fifty drivers, stablemen, innkeepers, and mechanics. For the westward trip he charged $200, which included forty pounds of baggage but neither meals nor lodging. For the eastward journey—probably because there was less demand—he charged at one time $100 and later $150.

If you were in a hurry, you could get from St. Louis to San Francisco in twenty-five days on Butterfield's line, but you would be forced to travel day and night to make it. You must sleep sitting up in a swaying, rocking coach, very likely with passengers on each side of you. Rather than go through such an ordeal, you would probably stop off along the way for a day or two at a time, and rest up.

Brown Brothers

Wagon train freighter using six pairs of horses.

Today, when a long freight train rumbles westbound through the plains of Nebraska, its cars loaded with merchandise manufactured in the East, the sight is so commonplace that you hardly raise your head. But you would have gazed in awe if you had seen how Russell, Majors, and Waddell freighted the same goods in the 1860's.

They had wagons capable of carrying five thousand pounds drawn by six pairs of mules or six yokes of oxen. These wagons wound their way across the prairies in convoys two miles long. At night the wagons were placed in a great circle with the men and stock camped inside, for protection against the Indians. Had you come to the crest of a hill and looked down upon the spot, you would have seen scores of campfires lighting the men, oxen, mules, and wagons, and had you inspected more closely you might have seen armed sentries outside the circle of wagons.

These wagon freighters served the growing mines and ranches of the Rockies with groceries, clothing, tools, and other items that pioneers need. The long overland trip was costly, and as a result the ordinary staples of life were high-priced to our first western families.

Brown Brothers

The main street of Helena, Montana, in 1869.

Potatoes frequently sold for as high as twenty-five cents a pound, a sack of flour twenty-five dollars, and a box of matches seventy-five cents. All because of the difficulties of transportation.

But while such services as these provided regular transportation for passengers and freight, some way was still necessary to send information quickly between East and West. Telegraph lines were reaching out from San Francisco toward the eastern boundary of the state. Other lines were being built into Nebraska from the east. Between these terminals were the open plains and mountains. Russell, Majors, and Waddell set out to bridge that gap in the only swift way possible.

They bought wiry ponies, hired sturdy young riders, and established a chain of relay stations across the plains between telegraph terminals. With horse and rider galloping day and night over the Rockies and through Indian country, they planned to furnish communication between New York and San Francisco in nine days! Which meant, actually, that they proposed to bridge the gap between eastern California and western Nebraska in nine days. To do it, they could allow the

Chicago Historical Society
Pony Bob of the Pony Express carried the news of Lincoln's election, one hundred and twenty miles in eight hours and ten minutes.

rider only two minutes at a relay station to throw his saddlebags, stuffed with mail, onto a fresh horse and be off.

This service is known in history as the Pony Express.

For eighteen months, until the telegraph line was completed across the continent, the Pony Express operated unfailingly. Letters were first carried for five dollars apiece, eventually one dollar. The service was twice-a-week. Buffalo Bill Cody was a Pony Express rider and it is said that once he rode continuously for twenty-two hours and covered three hundred and twenty miles.

In addition to the overland stage lines, freight wagon lines, and the Pony Express, regular service was provided between New York and San Francisco by the Pacific Mail Steamship Company. The trip took about a month. You went from New York to Chagres in Panama, and

there you took a short overland trip to Panama City along the trail followed by Morgan and his buccaneers in the days of the Spanish Main. At Panama you boarded another vessel for San Francisco.

All this time, steamboats were pushing farther and farther up the Missouri River until, in 1860, two boats—the *Chippewa* and *Key West*—reached Fort Benton in the Montana Rockies. Within a few years gold was discovered in various places in Montana, a horde of

men flowed into the valleys, and steamboats were busy bringing up clothing, guns, flour, salt, and the other necessities of life. In 1867 no fewer than thirty-nine steamboats docked at Fort Benton.

It must have been an unbelievable sight—those side-wheelers and stern-wheelers tied up along the bank in a mountain valley more than two thousand miles from the river's mouth at St. Louis!

Steamboating on the upper Missouri was to last until 1878 when railroad competition put an end to it. Stagecoaches were to retreat before the railroad, but were to be seen until 1900 in isolated parts of the West. But the beginning of the end for both came in 1863 when the Central Pacific in California and the Union Pacific in Nebraska began building toward each other with the ultimate objective of forming a continuous line of iron rails across the continent.

The starting point in the story of the building of the first transcontinental railroad is the arrival in California in 1854 of a young man named Theodore D. Judah. Judah was born in Bridgeport, Connecticut, in 1826 and studied engineering at Troy Polytechnic Institute, in New York. He had worked on several railroads in the East and was one of the young engineers called by California to help build railroads in that state.

But while Judah worked for the short Sacramento Valley line, he dreamed of a long railroad to the East. He explored the Sierra Nevada range in eastern California until he found a pass through which he was certain a railroad could be built. And, in 1859, at his own expense, he went to Washington to plead for national aid. There he received encouragement, and returned west to form a company and raise capital.

San Francisco capitalists were not interested, whereupon he went inland to Sacramento. There, finally, he gained the support of four men—Collis P. Huntington, Mark Hopkins, Leland Stanford, and Charles Crocker. Huntington and Hopkins were partners in a hardware store. Stanford was an ex-lawyer from New York who had sold miners' supplies for a time and received considerable money as his share in a mining project. In 1861 Stanford was to be elected gov-

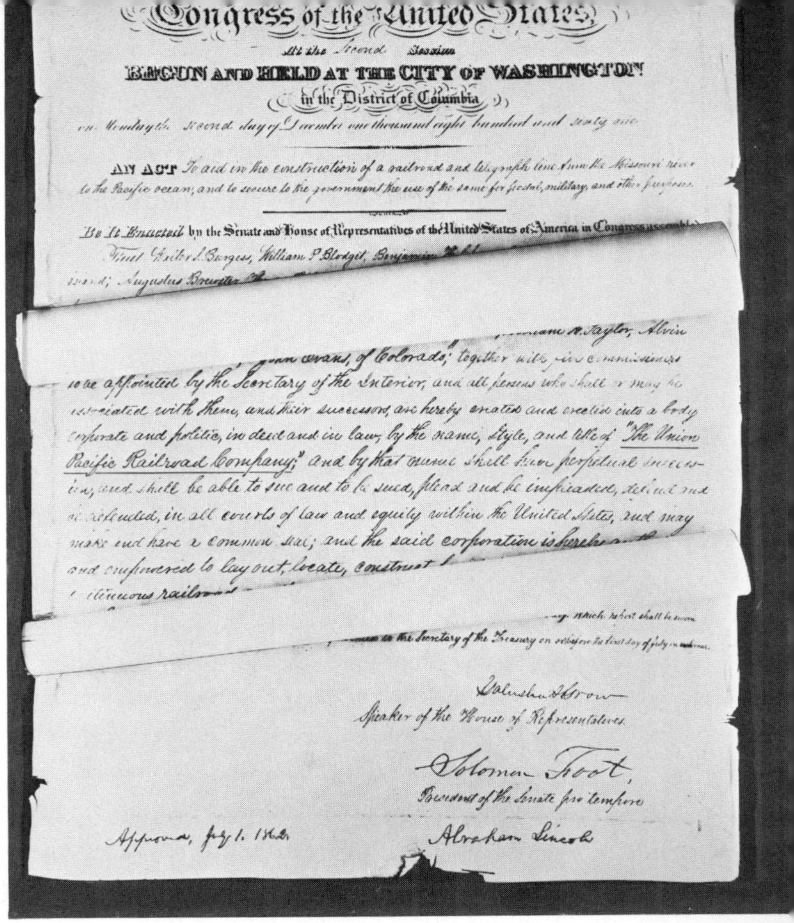
Congress of the United States,
At the Second Session
Begun and held at the City of Washington
in the District of Columbia
on Monday the second day of December one thousand eight hundred and sixty one
AN ACT To aid in the construction of a railroad and telegraph line from the Missouri river to the Pacific ocean; and to secure to the government the use of the same for postal, military, and other purposes.
Be It Enacted by the Senate and House of Representatives of the United States of America in Congress assembled
Walter S. Burgess, William P. Blodget, Benjamin
Augustus Brewster
Taylor, Alvin
John Evans, of Colorado; together with five commissioners to be appointed by the Secretary of the Interior, and all persons who shall or may be associated with them, and their successors, are hereby created and erected into a body corporate and politic, in deed and in law, by the name, style, and title of "The Union Pacific Railroad Company;" and by that name shall have perpetual succession, and shall be able to sue and to be sued, plead and be impleaded, defend and be defended, in all courts of law and equity within the United States, and may make and have a common seal; and the said corporation is hereby
and empowered to lay out, locate, construct
continuous railroad
which report shall be sworn
to the Secretary of the Treasury on or before the first day of July in each year.
Galusha A. Grow
Speaker of the House of Representatives.
Solomon Foot,
President of the Senate pro tempore
Approved, July 1, 1862.
Abraham Lincoln

Congressional deed and title to the Union Pacific Railroad Company.
Union Pacific Railroad

ernor of California. Charles Crocker was a miner, trader, and alderman of Sacramento.

These four men formed the Central Pacific Railroad with a California charter dated June 28, 1861, elected officers, and paid in enough money to give the company legal status. They appointed Judah chief engineer. And in 1861, Judah went back to Washington to tell the government that the railroad was organized, and how about some help?

A railroad the size of the proposed Central Pacific could not be built by four Sacramento businessmen of limited means. Governmental aid was needed. Judah's mission to Washington was highly successful. The aid offered the Central Pacific was exceedingly generous.

The United States agreed to lend the company $16,000 per mile for that part of the line built on level ground, $32,000 per mile for somewhat more difficult terrain, and $48,000 per mile for mountain sections. In addition, from the public lands, the company was deeded twenty sections of land per mile of railroad. From the direct loan the railroad eventually was to realize $20,735,000, and from the sale of land over the years that followed it was to receive about $10,000,000. In addition it received varying loans from the state, and from towns that would be helped by the road.

In the building not only of this road, but others, great sums of money came into the hands of the controlling stockholders. Yet interest on these loans must be paid, and some day the bonds must be paid in full. It appears that the stockholders had no great confidence in the ability of those early roads to make good these obligations. So most of them decided to make their money out of building the railroad itself.

They formed construction companies and gave these companies the contract to build the road. The same men controlled both the construction company and the railroad company. As railroad directors, they gave the construction company the job of building the road at prices that would guarantee the construction company a substantial profit. As directors of the construction company, they built the road and declared themselves handsome dividends. Thus the borrowed money went through the railroad and the construction company into the pockets of the controlling directors.

This was not good for the railroads because it resulted in too-high building costs, but it was very good for the insiders. Many of them grew exceedingly rich. Before we leave the subject of finances, however, we should point out one justification for the construction company. The government, in turning over bonds to the railroad, had required the railroad to sell the bonds to the public at par.

But it is not easy to sell a hundred-dollar bond at par because investors wish to make a little extra profit. They might buy a hundred-dollar bond at ninety, they would be even more eager to buy it at eighty, but why buy it at par when it was so easy to get rich in other ways? The result was that the railroad had bonds which the public was slow in buying. And if the public would not buy them, how could the railroad get the money to lay its track?

So the insiders let the railroad pay the bonds to the construction company for work done. To protect themselves they made the prices of the work so high that the construction company could make a profit even if it was forced to sell those bonds for eighty or ninety. There was no objection to the construction company's selling the bonds for any price it could get—it was asked only that the railroad sell them at par.

Financial matters are frequently troublesome, but they are an important part in the building of our transportation system. Bonds and construction companies were part of the machinery whereby the savings and credit of the nation were poured into the shining steel rails that stretched eastward through canyons and tunnels in the Sierra Nevada Mountains.

The human and physical side of railroad building is more romantic than the financial side. And the physical problems of building the Central Pacific were staggering.

Building the railroad across the Great Plains.

Hudson Historical Bureau

There was the question of materials and supplies. Rails, tieplate, spikes, and tools had to come by ship from the east, the lighter materials by way of the Isthmus of Panama, and the heavier materials such as rolling stock all the way around South America. Rails that cost $91.70 per ton in the East mounted to $143.67 when shipped via Panama.

The labor question was just as serious. Few men wished to work on a railroad when the opportunities for wealth in mining, farming, and storekeeping seemed so rosy. In 1864 the Central Pacific was able to find only 1,200 men willing to work for it. Finally the builders solved the problem by importing Chinese coolies who were willing to work for thirty-five dollars a month and board themselves. The white laborers received thirty-five dollars and were boarded by the railroad. By 1867 the railroad was employing 14,500 white laborers and coolies, and work was moving swiftly ahead.

Meanwhile, from the east, the Union Pacific was unrolling across

Cheyenne Indians attacking hand-car crew, 1869.

Union Pacific Railroad

Union Pacific Railroad

Woodburning locomotive, 1867.

the plains. It had been chartered by Congress on July 1, 1862, about a year after the chartering of the Central Pacific. It received the same aid as the Central Pacific. By the same construction-company device, government bonds were made available for building—and for enriching the promoters. It was using the same gauge track—four feet eight and one-half inches—and this gauge was to become standard all over the country, so that eventually the cars of one road could ride on the tracks of all roads.

The Union Pacific broke ground at Omaha in December, 1863, and started slowly across the plains. It had almost as much difficulty getting material as the Central Pacific. Supplies were mainly carried by boat up the Missouri and hauled out to the line on wagons. Few men were available for work because most able-bodied men were fighting in the Civil War, and the Union Pacific didn't go so far as to import Chinese labor. As a result, in 1864–65 only forty miles of track were laid.

At the end of the war, with discharged soldiers available for work, track laying went faster. The line stretched out into Indian country and men worked with armed troops guarding them or with rifles stacked handy, so that they could drop their shovels and pick up guns in case raiding parties swept down on them. In spite of all the protection, Indians stole horses, burned camps, tore up tracks, and captured and killed workmen.

By July, 1866, the road was completed to Kearney, Nebraska, 305

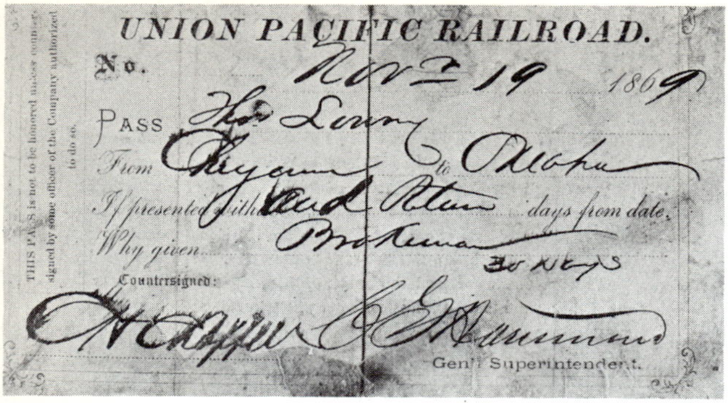
UNION PACIFIC RAILROAD.
No. Nov 19 1869
PASS
From to
If presented with days from date.
Why given
Countersigned:
Gen'l Superintendent.
THIS PASS is not to be honored unless countersigned by some officer of the Company authorized to do so.

Railroad pass, 1869.
Union Pacific Railroad

miles west of Omaha, and the young line was opened for business with a fare of ten cents per mile.

In the winter of 1867–68 the Union Pacific reached Cheyenne and began racing the Central Pacific to see which road could build farthest and get the most government assistance. For Congress had specified no particular meeting place. It had only guaranteed to lend money ranging from $16,000 to $48,000 per mile for each mile completed. Both roads realized that each mile built meant that much more money in the coffers, and each road intended to take as much of the premium as it could.

They whipped themselves into racing speed, and their road building became heroic for its feverish pace if not for its excellence. Observers marveled at the way in which track was laid.

First went the graders working with scrapers, pick and shovel, cutting through hills and filling in hollows, laying a smooth, narrow bed of earth and gravel.

Then came the ties, cut by gangs in the forests of the Black Hills

Construction train, 1867.
Union Pacific Railroad

Santa Fe Railway

"Solid oak ties, and rail weighing fifty-six pounds to the yard!" Laying rail on the Santa Fe.

and on the slopes of the Rockies and hauled by team to the roadbed, where they were swiftly set in place.

After that the rails, and this part amazed all watchers. Back at the supply depot the rails were loaded on horse-drawn trucks, the wheels of which were flanged to fit the track. These truck loads of rails, with tieplates and spikes, were driven at a gallop down the road to the end of the track.

There gangs pulled the rails off the wagons, carried them forward, and at a signal lowered them to the track. Rail after rail was carried forward and put in place until the truck was unloaded.

The empty truck was then dumped over on its side, off the track, to allow the next loaded truck to pass it at a gallop, on down the new sections of track already bolted in place. When the loaded truck had passed, the empty one was lifted onto the rails again and driven back to the supply depot.

Dale Creek Bridge, first erected entirely of wood in only thirty working days, was later replaced by a bridge of steel.
Union Pacific Railroad

Using these methods, the Union Pacific laid four to seven miles of track per day, and on record-breaking days ten miles. Into the winter of 1868–69, without calling a halt for cold weather, they worked at breakneck speed.

By the spring of 1869 both companies were working in western Utah, Chinese coolies laying track eastward on the Central Pacific, Irish laborers and ex-soldiers sweating westward on the Union Pacific. Day by day they came closer until they were within hailing distance, and finally, on parallel roadbeds, within a stone's throw, they began passing each other, the Central Pacific blithely laying track eastward and the Union Pacific just as unconcernedly laying track toward the west.

It seems incredible, but it is a fact that these two railroads, supposed to effect a meeting, went right on building track as though the other did not exist. In their eagerness to dig into the federal treasury, both roads apparently intended to keep on building until stopped by the oceans.

To remedy the oversight, Congress designated Promontory Point, Utah, as the meeting place, and there, on May 10, 1869, the two roads performed the ceremony of completing the first transcontinental railroad. The Central Pacific had laid 689 miles of track eastward from Sacramento, over the Sierra Nevada Mountains, and the Union Pacific had laid 1,086 miles westward from Omaha, through Indian country and over the Rockies.

The telegraph had kept pace with the roads, and now, on that historic spring day, the singing wires were to carry to the world the story of the placing of the last tie and the driving of the last few spikes.

The tie was a piece of laurel wood from California. It was placed on the roadbed. The last two rails were put down.

Seventeen spikes would be needed to hold the two rails in place—ten spikes for one rail, seven for the other. Three of these spikes were unusual. Nevada contributed a spike of silver, Arizona a spike of iron, silver, and gold, and California a spike of pure gold.

Over the tapping telegraph keys the message sped to cities and

Union Pacific Railroad

The Central Pacific and Union Pacific are joined.

villages throughout the United States where citizens had gathered in the squares in honor of the event:

"Almost ready . . . Hats off . . . Prayer is being offered."

And while the Irish laborers, Chinese coolies, Mexicans, Indians, and silk-hatted officials formed a colorful band at the actual spot, masses of citizens bared their heads, from coast to coast.

Union Pacific Railroad

Then, in dot-dash: "The spike is about to be presented."

A little later: "All is ready now."

Finally, as the spikes of silver and gold were driven home the telegrapher signaled each blow of the sledge, and these self-same blows were recorded in every city by the ringing of a bell.

Had there been television then, the entire ceremony would have been visible on screens in every living room in the nation, but the telegraph was marvel enough, and people must have felt, as they listened to the tolling bells, that they were themselves out in Utah, watching the welding of the last link in America's most daring, romantic epoch of railroad building.

ACROSS THE CONTINENT.
"WESTWARD THE COURSE OF EMPIRE TAKES ITS WAY."

13 · RAILROADS COVER THE NATION, BECOME REGULATED, AND GROW SAFER

In 1870, the year after the completion of the Union Pacific-Central Pacific, the United States had 52,922 miles of railroad, enough to go twice around the world. That is a tremendous record of growth when you consider that there were only 9,000 miles of railroad in 1850, but it was the merest warning of the building that was to take place in the next twenty years.

By 1880, in spite of the fact that the country went through a six-year depression—the worst depression it had ever suffered—railway mileage had increased to 93,262. During the next decade, the United States went into a fever of grading and track laying such as the world had neven seen. No fewer than 70,000 miles of railroad were added, bringing the total mileage in 1890 to 163,597.

Most of these new roads were being built in the West, and were an important part of the miracle that was changing the West from a frontier to a settled country. Wherever the railroads went, they opened up new sources of wealth. The wheat of the Dakotas, the cattle of Texas and Wyoming, the gold, copper, silver, and lead of the Rocky Mountain regions had a new way of getting to market.

And as new farms were settled and new mines opened, new towns sprang up on the railroads. Hamlets and sleepy cow towns grew into

Shooting buffalo from the engine.

Union Pacific Railroad

Topeka, Kansas, in 1870.

bustling cities. The number of people west of the Mississippi in 1870 was only seven million; in 1890 it was seventeen million.

And the cities! Kansas City leaped from 3,000 in 1880 to 37,000 in 1890! Denver from 5,000 in 1870 to 107,000 in 1890! Omaha from 16,000 in 1870 to 140,000 in 1890! Salt Lake City from 13,000 in 1870 to 45,000 in 1890!

In the Southwest, where shiny new transcontinental rails stretched across the plains and deserts, Dallas went from 10,000 in 1880 to 38,000 in 1890; San Antonio from 12,000 in 1870 to 38,000 in 1890.

Railroad depot, Omaha, Nebraska.

Union Pacific Railroad

Up north, Minneapolis leaped from 13,000 in 1870 to 164,000 in 1890 and St. Paul from 20,000 to 133,000 in the same time. At the other end of the line, Seattle mushroomed from 3,500 in 1880 to 42,000 in 1890.

Thus the growth of the great railroads in the West was also the growth of great cities. New states, too, were admitted in a swift procession: Nevada in 1864, with the Central Pacific crawling toward it; Nebraska in 1867, with the Union Pacific bisecting it; Colorado in 1876; North and South Dakota, Montana, and Washington, all in 1889; Idaho and Wyoming in 1890.

Only six states were still to be admitted after 1890—Utah, Arizona, New Mexico, Oklahoma, Alaska, and Hawaii. The country was settled to the whistle and smoke of railroad locomotives.

But while railroads were performing the great service of settling the West, some of their activities aroused great indignation. Most of this indignation was due to the way in which freight rates were charged.

If you were a manufacturer and wished to ship a certain kind of cloth from New York to San Francisco, the cost was $1.00 per hundred pounds. But if you wished to ship the same amount to Salt Lake City, the cost was $2.30 per hundred pounds. It frequently cost more to ship goods a shorter distance than it did a longer one.

There was a reason for it. Between New York and San Francisco there was water competition. If the railroads charged too much, the manufacturer could send his goods by boat by way of Panama. But there was no boat service to Salt Lake City.

Union Pacific No. 1, the *General Sherman*, a woodburner. Built in Paterson, New Jersey, in 1864-65 and brought to Omaha by steamboat in June, 1865.

Union Pacific Railroad

One Rochester, New York, man found that if he shipped his goods east to New York City, and then west—right back through Rochester—to Cincinnati, it cost fourteen cents less per hundred pounds than if he shipped direct to Cincinnati.

This was called "local discrimination" and the people who suffered did not like it, even though the railroads pointed out that they were forced to charge high rates wherever they could, in order to keep from going bankrupt.

There was another kind of discrimination called personal discrimination and this was less excusable. In 1885, an Ohio railroad charged the Standard Oil Company ten cents per barrel to ship oil from Macksburg, Ohio, to Marietta, Ohio. The same railroad charged smaller independents thirty-five cents per barrel and actually turned over to the Standard Oil Company the extra twenty-five cents. In other words, the railroad was co-operating with one company to drive other companies out of business.

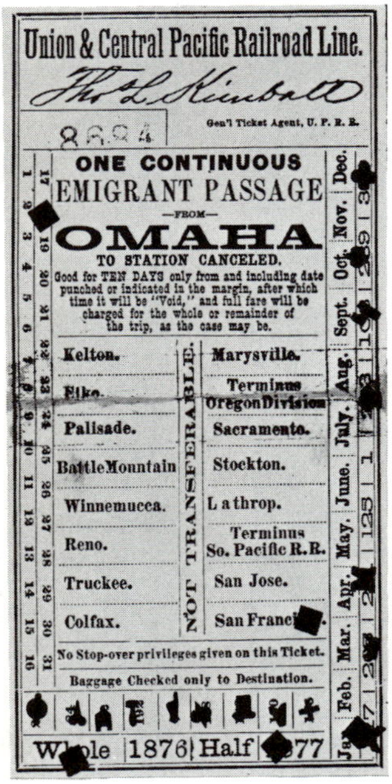

Union Pacific Railroad

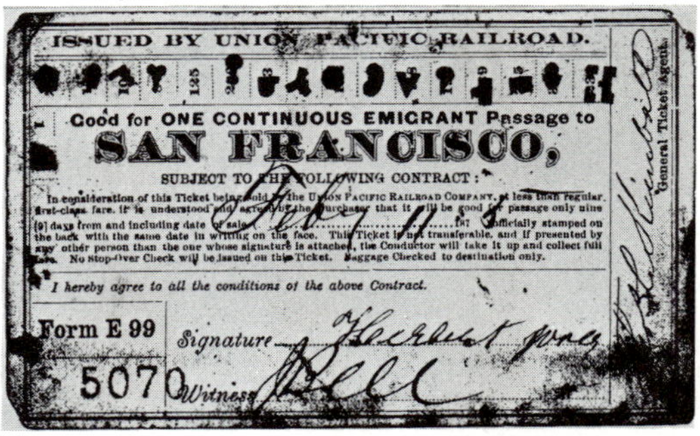

These matters caused so much protest that in 1887 Congress passed the Act to Regulate Commerce and created the Interstate Commerce Commission to administer it. The object of the Act, and of the amendments that have increased its power since 1887, is to regulate rates and guarantee fair treatment as between shippers, and as between localities.

So the period of the railroad's greatest growth also saw it come under the regulation of the United States government. And the same period saw the introduction of the greatest contribution to railroad safety—the automatic air brake.

Shortly after the Civil War, two trains collided head-on between Troy and Schenectady, in New York state. Although the damage in battered and crushed rolling stock was heavy, this was one of the most fortunate accidents that could have befallen the railroad because one of the observers at the scene was a restless, mechanically minded young man named George Westinghouse.

Westinghouse had packed considerable experience into his twenty years of life. He had served as a cavalryman and naval engineer in the Civil War. He had gone to Union College in Schenectady for a while but had left because he could interest himself in nothing but machinery. As long as he could remember he had tinkered with machines in the Schenectady shop where his father designed and built farm equipment. As a boy he had even designed a rotary engine. Now, as a young man, he was already building and selling a car replacer—a device for hauling derailed cars back on the track.

On this day when he gazed at the overturned cars, all his professional curiosity was aroused. He could see little excuse for a collision. The day was clear and the track was level. Somebody must have been extremely careless.

"What was the matter?" he asked a trainman. "Wouldn't the brakes work?"

"Sure, but there wasn't time. You can't stop a train in a moment."

The remark brought home to Westinghouse the inefficiency of the brake system then in use. When an engineer wished to stop his train, he signaled with his whistle. The brakeman, standing on the platform of a car, tightened the brakes by turning a wheel, thereby drawing a chain taut and setting the brake shoes. Then the brakeman stepped across to the other platform and turned another wheel. Farther down the train other brakemen did the same thing.

The engineers of the wrecked trains had undoubtedly whistled "brakes down" as soon as they saw each other, but before the necessary braking could be done the trains had come together with enough force to cause a bad wreck.

"If an engineer had some way of setting the brakes from the cab instead of depending on a crew of men," Westinghouse thought, "wrecks like this could be avoided."

Why wouldn't it be possible to have a single chain running from

Railroad wreck, 1871.

Old engraving

the locomotive down the length of the train? Then, if the engineer had some way of taking up the slack on the chain, he could set the brakes on all cars at once.

He discussed the idea with railroad men and found that the Burlington Railroad already had such a brake in use. It was the best brake so far designed. A single chain was attached to the brakes on all cars and to a windlass in the engine. The windlass could be brought into contact with the driving wheel of the locomotive, so that the friction would turn the windlass, draw up the chain, and set the brakes.

The chief trouble with the idea, as Westinghouse saw it, was that a long train would need a tremendously large windlass.

He wondered if steam power could not be utilized to set brakes, but rejected the idea almost at once. By the time you conveyed steam through long pipes it would condense and the power would be lost.

One day, while he was eating lunch, a woman sold him a subscription to a magazine called *Living Age*. Glancing idly through the copy she left with him, he became interested in a story describing the boring of the Mont Cenis tunnel in Switzerland. Compressed air had been used to drive the rock drills, the compressed air traveling through long pipes from a machine at the tunnel mouth.

As he read the article, his eyes lighted in sudden triumph. Here was the answer to the brake puzzle! If compressed air could be conveyed through long pipes without losing its power to do work, then it could be used to set brakes on a train.

From that time on, he could think of nothing but the air brake that was taking shape in his mind. He moved to Pittsburgh, designed his air brake, and with money advanced by a friend built enough braking equipment for a short train.

Then came a series of discouraging rebuffs. Every railroad he approached agreed that the brake was ingenious. Not one, however, was willing to spend the money for a test. "We'll lend you a locomotive and cars," several of them said, "but you'll have to install the brakes at your own expense."

Finally, with more borrowed money, Westinghouse equipped a four-car train belonging to the Panhandle Railroad and invited railroad men to watch the demonstration. Judged by present-day standards his device was primitive.

On the engine he had an air pump and a reservoir in which to store the compressed air. Pipes led from the reservoir to cylinders on the four cars. By moving a valve handle the engineer could send air through the pipes to the cylinders, thus operating pistons and setting the brakes.

The train pulled out of the Pittsburgh station with Westinghouse and the observers aboard. It had not gone far when the untried brakes were called upon for an unexpected test. At a street crossing, a drayman drove his horse and wagon onto the track in front of the train. The horses took fright and lunged. The drayman toppled from his seat, fell to the ground, and lay unconscious across the tracks.

The engineer of the test train applied the air brakes, and the train screeched to a stop so abruptly that the passengers inside the coaches were thrown out of their seats. At first they were inclined to be irritated at the rough treatment, but when they discovered that a tragedy had been averted, they looked at young Westinghouse with new respect. A more severe test could scarcely have been planned. The brake had stood up.

After this test it was easy to raise money to build a factory, and thus it happened that in 1869, at the age of twenty-three, George Westinghouse found himself at the head of a company capitalized at a half million dollars—the Westinghouse Air Brake Company.

But his troubles were only commencing. For twenty years he was to find fault with his own product and labor to improve it. That first air brake, for instance. What would happen if the train parted and a pipe broke? The air would leak out and the train would be without brakes.

To overcome that objection he designed a brake that would automatically set itself whenever the air pressure was *reduced*. Thus, if a train broke and air escaped from the pipes, valves would be actuated

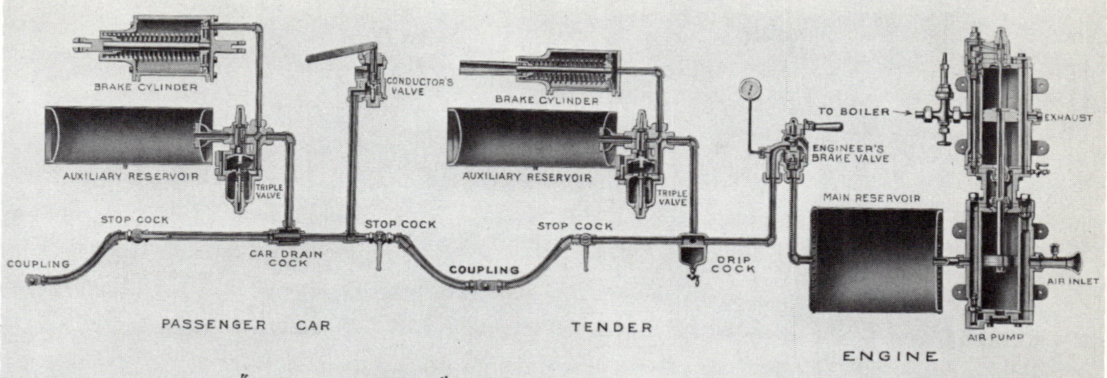

THE "WESTINGHOUSE" PLAIN AUTOMATIC AIR BRAKE 1872.

and reservoirs on each car would go into action, setting the brakes.

Then came tests in 1886 and 1887 at Burlington, Iowa, in which all manufacturers of brakes were invited to compete, so that railroads could determine once and for all what brake to recommend for standard equipment on all lines. Brakes actuated by electricity and by vacuum were entered, and Westinghouse submitted a combined air and electric brake.

The air and electric brake did well enough, but Westinghouse did not dare trust to electricity. Suppose a wire broke or a connection came loose? The train would be without brakes.

So he went back to his all-air brake. The trouble with it, he found, was that on a long freight train it did not act simultaneously on all cars. The brakes were set successively from front to rear, with the result that the rear cars banged into the cars ahead, causing considerable damage. How could the brake be made satisfactory for long trains?

There was no royal road to the answer. By enlarging a valve here, redesigning a part there, by making small improvements wherever improvements were possible, Westinghouse finally achieved a design that would set the brakes on a fifty-car train almost instantaneously.

Air brake cylinder.

Railroad men proclaimed his brake the best in existence. Only the Westinghouse brake satisfied the rigid requirements of railroad men.

Thus, over a long period of hard work, Westinghouse triumphed. Such accidents as he had witnessed as a young man near Schenectady, where two trains on a straight stretch of road, a long distance apart, were unable to stop in time to avoid a collision, were forever eliminated from the scene.

The air brake was not Westinghouse's only contribution to rail-

Brake shoe of freight car.

roading. He manufactured switching and signaling apparatus. But the air brake was his first, and undoubtedly his greatest, contribution to railroad safety.

About the same time that Westinghouse witnessed the head-on collision near Schenectady that started him off on the invention of the air brake, railroad men were looking for a safe and sure way of holding trains together.

There had been considerable development in couplers since the *DeWitt Clinton* had blithely set out from Albany on July 30, 1831, hauling a little train of cars joined together by lengths of chain. The coupler in general use during the Civil War was known as the link-and-pin, which was successful in holding cars together, but was exceedingly dangerous to trainmen. To couple a pair of cars, a man had to go between the cars and raise the link so that it would enter the link pocket on the other car as the cars came together.

Hundreds of trainmen were maimed or crushed to death each year doing this job. Men so injured were generally given jobs as crossing watchmen, and the sight of a watchman with part of a hand or a stub for arm was common. Men tried to conquer this problem by devising a coupler that would work automatically, without the necessity of a trainman going between the cars.

Link and pin coupler.
Union Pacific Railroad

In 1863, the Miller hooks appeared. These were simply a pair of iron hooks at the ends of long shanks, held in line by springs. Miller hooks were a forward step, but they had a tendency to become disengaged through sidewise movement. This fault wasn't solved until a dignified Virginia farmer named Eli Janney returned from the Civil War and went to work on the problem.

The story goes that Major Janney locked his cupped hands together and studied them to see what could be done to keep the curved fingers from slipping out to the sides. In a moment of revelation he placed his thumbs so that they embraced the outside of his fingers. He saw instantly that his question was answered.

The thumbs, acting as guard arms, plus a pivoting knuckle that could be locked in the cupped position, gave Janney the basic idea of the modern car coupler. He patented his invention in 1866.

The coupler was successful from the first and gained national acceptance when the Westinghouse Air Brake Company, in 1882, sent a fifty-car train around the country to demonstrate its compressed-air brake. The train was equipped with Janney couplers, and authorities state that it was the ability of the Janney coupler to hold a train tightly together that made the air brake possible.

In 1893, Congress passed an act requiring all cars used in interstate commerce to be equipped with automatic couplers, and by 1905 the changeover was complete.

The first locomotive equipped with compressed air power brakes for regular railroad service, 1869.

Westinghouse Air Brake Co.

With the automatic coupler, cars could be uncoupled by an operating lever that extended to the side of the freight car. Similarly, when cars came together, the lock that held the knuckle in the gripping position dropped into place automatically. Though the design didn't always work perfectly, with the result that men sometimes still went between the cars, the rate of accidents due to coupling dropped so dramatically that one national magazine called the automatic coupler "the greatest lifesaver ever invented."

Santa Fe Railway

14 · RAILROAD TRANSPORTATION TODAY

OUR country's railroads, in meeting the triple threat of air lanes, highways, and waterways, have made great technical strides in recent years. Let's sit down in one of the most modern of today's trains, take a fast trip over the countryside, and see what we can learn about present-day railroading.

Dining car, 1875.
Canadian National Railways

We have approximately 220,000 miles of railroad, or somewhat over one-fourth of the world's mileage. In the heyday of railroading we had 250,000 miles, but, as trucks and busses have taken over part of the transportation task, many branch lines have been discontinued. Our passengers and freight are carried by 33,000 passenger cars and 1,750,000 freight cars, with 35,000 locomotives to do the pulling.

The train in which you are riding bears little resemblance to the heavy black trains of the early 1930's. This one is built of stainless steel, which is rustproof and stronger than conventional steel.

The bright, gleaming exterior of this train is just as shiny as it was on the day it was put into service. The fourteen cars and two Diesel locomotive units weigh a grand total of 1,300 tons, where an old-

Interior of parlor car, 1906.

fashioned steel train of the same size would have weighed over 2,000 tons.

As you walk through the train, you notice much that is different. All cars are, of course, air-conditioned and heat-controlled. But the colors! As you pass from car to car, your eye is pleasantly captured by soft shades of rose, green, pink, tan, and blue. The effect is bright and cheerful, as compared to the somber tones of older trains.

Your grandfathers never heard of a low-cost diner with a lunch counter, but this train has one. It is called the "Chuck Wagon," with one-half of it taken up by the spotless counter of stainless steel and one-half of it by a coffee shop. There's also a dining car, somewhat more elegant and more conventional.

Three of the cars in the train are equipped with sightseer's domes for travelers who like to have an unimpeded view of the mountains and canyons. These domes are bubbles of clear, nonglare safety glass under which passengers sit in deep-cushioned seats.

Sleeping arrangements have undergone a radical change. The old first-class Pullmans with upper and lower berths have been rapidly disappearing from the scene. They have been succeeded by roomette cars, each roomette with its individual washbasin and toilet. For passengers willing to pay more, there are staterooms and drawing rooms. The inconvenience of leaving your berth in the morning and walking down a public aisle to the washroom, with clothes draped over your arm, is becoming a memory.

Our train has, in addition to dining cars and Pullman sleepers, four day coaches, an observation lounge, a mail-and-baggage car, and an express car.

At our first stop, we walk forward along the platform to have a look at the powerful Diesels. They bear little resemblance to the giant steam locomotives that first conquered time and distance for our nation. The exterior is unmarred by pistons, cylinders, and high driving wheels. No bells, domes, or stack interrupt the smooth contour of the top. There is no coal tender at the rear.

The Diesel is a low, sleek monster with small wheels and a bluntly rounded front end. Its stainless steel body is as bright as the coaches. Inside each unit are two Diesel engines of 1,200 horsepower each, making a total of 4,800 horsepower in the two units. These engines drive generators, which supply electricity to traction motors mounted on the axles. In other words, this train is electrically driven, the locomotive making its own electricity as it goes along.

It took only twenty-five years for the powerful, unromantic Diesel to drive steam off the railroads of the nation. How could so complete a transformation have taken place in so short a time?

The Diesel is an outgrowth of the rail car, which had a gasoline-electric unit in the front end, with the rest of the car devoted to passengers and baggage. Its power unit operated on the same principle as that in the big locomotive beside you. During the 1920's there were over five hundred rail cars in use on short branch lines, carrying passengers and small freight between cities.

Because rail cars proved their economy on short lines, railroad men decided to introduce them to the main line. This happened during the memorable summer of 1934, when two brand-new trains were presented to the public.

One of them, the *City of Salina,* belonged to the Union Pacific. It was a three-car streamliner built of aluminum. Its cars were "articulated," meaning that the rear end of one car and the head end of the next car were mounted on the same four-wheel truck. The power car at the front end looked like a small version of the present-day Diesel

City of Salina.

Union Pacific Railroad

locomotive. It contained a 600-horsepower engine burning a kind of low-grade gasoline called distillate.

The other train was the *Pioneer Zephyr,* owned by the Burlington lines. It was also a three-car streamliner, but it was built of stainless steel rather than aluminum, and its engine was an eight-cylinder Diesel, built by the Winton plant of General Motors and rated at 600 horsepower. This engine was the true ancestor of the locomotives that pull our trains today.

These trains introduced the bright colors and streamlined design found in trains today. They represented the railroads' attempt to win passengers in the face of competition from buses and the two-engine air liners that were beginning to criss-cross the skies at speeds of 180 miles per hour.

To dramatize their speed, both lines staged sensational test runs. On May 26, 1934, the *Pioneer Zephyr* made its famous dawn-to-dusk run from Denver to Chicago. The fastest steam schedule for the trip was twenty-six hours. The *Zephyr* made it in exactly thirteen hours and five minutes, averaging 78 miles per hour over the 1,015 miles! Aboard was a small Rocky Mountain burro, presented by the people of Denver to the people of Chicago.

In October of the same year, the Union Pacific staged a test run with its second streamliner, the *M-10001,* a five-car articulated train powered by a 900-horsepower Diesel. On October 22 the *M-10001* left Los Angeles for New York in an attempt to set a new transcontinental record.

The old record was claimed by the fabulous gold prospector, Death Valley Scotty, who had chartered a special Santa Fe train in 1905 and made the run from Los Angeles to Chicago in forty-four hours, fifty-four minutes, using nineteen steam locomotives en route.

The *M-10001* made the first 144 miles through the Sierra Madre Mountains in three hours and six minutes, an hour and a half faster than the steam schedule. It sped through the Rockies, showing exceptional power on the grades.

From Cheyenne, Wyoming, to Omaha, Nebraska, the track ran

level, and down this stretch the gleaming train hurtled at speeds that reached 120 miles an hour.

The run to Chicago was finished in thirty-eight hours, forty-nine minutes, breaking Death Valley Scotty's record by over six hours, after which the *M-10001* continued to New York at sedate steam schedules, completing the transcontinental crossing in the record time of fifty-six hours and fifty-five minutes.

Exploits such as these stirred the imagination of the public and encouraged other railroad lines to try out the new motive power. Diesel-electric locomotives moved out onto the main line, first hauling passenger cars, then freight trains.

It wasn't long before the railroads discovered just how efficient these quiet new locomotives were. Where a steam train had to change locomotives six or seven times between Chicago and the West Coast, a single Diesel-electric could go the entire way, then turn around and come back.

A steam locomotive had to fill its boilers at tanks stationed forty to fifty miles apart along the track. The Diesel needed only enough water to cool its engine, and therefore had to make no water stops at all.

A steam locomotive had to refuel frequently at coal chutes. A Diesel could run long distances without refueling. Those small railroad towns with their coal chutes and water tanks have become ghost towns on the American countryside. The familiar roundhouses have all but disappeared, too, giving way to neat, factory-type, Diesel repair shops.

Engineers liked the new Diesels after the strangeness had worn off. For many an old-time steam engineer, that first trip in a Diesel was an unnerving experience. Instead of leaning out the window, with one hand on the throttle, he sat in a cushioned armchair. He looked through a windshield, with windshield wiper and defroster to keep vision clear in rain or snow. There were no long boilers in front of him—only a rounded nose and the track. There were no coal dust, no firebox door, no breezes whipping in the open windows.

Union Pacific Railroad

His clothes would be almost as spotless at the end of the run as at the beginning.

Across from him sat his fireman, whose principal task would be to go back into the engine compartment and check a few gauges and dials.

The very ease and comfort of the engine cab were unsettling to the mind, but when the engineer put hand to throttle to start the train, the sensation was most unnerving of all. He could hear only the muffled sound of engines revving up behind him. No chug-chug of steam, no jerks as driving wheels slipped and caught. He opened the throttle wider and the muffled whine increased slightly—but no movement!

Then, if he looked outside, he saw that the station platform was beginning to slide backward. The train had got under way noiselessly, easily, at no particular instant, but only when the axles had gathered enough energy to turn the wheels. Such smooth, imperceptible starts were invariably a shock to those first Diesel engineers.

Something romantic was lost to the United States when the steam locomotive departed the scene, along with its plume of smoke and its drawn-out whistle. But the Diesel with its small wheels and its raucous horn is vastly more efficient. There were fifteen thousand fewer locomotives in the United States in 1955 than there were in 1935, but these thirty-five thousand Diesels did more work with less fuss than the fifty thousand steam locomotives of twenty years before.

The two Diesels hauling your luxury passenger train weigh slightly over 160 tons each, or a combined weight of about 320 tons. The first engines built in this country for the B. & O. weighed three and one-half tons. The *Stourbridge Lion,* imported from England, weighed seven tons.

Four old-timers that crossed the continent in the early days of railroading.

But we can't spend all our time up front, learning about engines, so walk back past the mail-and-baggage car—a miniature traveling post office in which mail is sorted en route—past the day coaches with their reclining seats. One of these coaches is called a "slumber coach" because its seats can be converted into small versions of the roomette for sleeping. Even coach fare passengers can have their private bedrooms at night!

As you walk back toward your car you glance at the track upon which the train wheels rest. It is made of rolled steel and weighs, most likely, around 115 pounds per yard. Our earlier rails in this country were made of cast iron. When Sir Henry Bessemer in the 1850's reduced the time of steelmaking from eight hours to fifteen minutes, thereby making steel cheap, it was possible to use steel for rails. The first steel rails used in this country lasted fifteen times as long as the iron!

The heavy rails rest on crossties of creosoted wood and the ties in turn rest on a crushed rock, gravel, or cinder bed called ballast. Rains soak quickly through a porous roadbed of this type, thus preventing washouts.

But the brakeman is saying, "All aboard!" It's time to be moving through the country, to learn what else we can about railroading.

Across the fields on that track heading northeast, a long freight train is moving. Motor trucks, waterways, and pipelines have increased steadily in importance over the years, but railroads still carry almost one-half of the freight in this country.

A three-unit Diesel of perhaps 6,000 horsepower may pull a hundred freight cars totaling a mile in length, and in that length we see cars of every kind and belonging to many railroads.

Here are yellow refrigerator cars. Unlike most boxcars, they have no sliding doors, but swinging doors that may be tightly shut. The sides of the cars are built of two layers of steel or wood with an insulating material in between. The car is cooled by circulating brine, or by ice tanks at either end of the car, or even, perhaps, by mechanical refrigerators just like the refrigerator in your house. Where your

Union Pacific Railroad

This 8500 horsepower engine pulls a train that seems to extend as far as the eye can see.

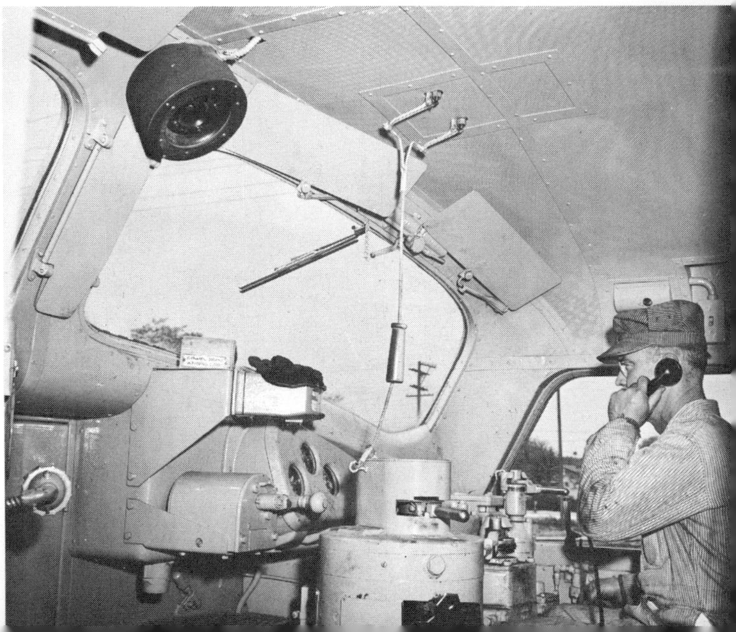

Sending a message to the caboose.
Santa Fe Railway

home refrigerator plugs into the house current for power to run the compressor, the refrigerator car is powered with its own small engine. In these refrigerator cars, the inside temperature can be held at any level down to ten below zero, and icing stops are not necessary.

The refrigerator car has caused great changes in the way meat is supplied to the American table. Before the development of the refrigerator car by Gustavus Swift in the 1870's, meat could not be carried any considerable distance without spoiling. Therefore live cattle had to be sent east and butchered in small packing plants close to the ultimate buyer. There had to be a packing plant in almost every town.

With the refrigerator car, meat could be safely shipped thousands of miles, thus making it possible to concentrate large packing plants in a few centers such as Chicago, Omaha, and Kansas City. Refrigerator cars made possible the rise of our great, centralized stockyards and packing houses.

In recent times, the trend has been reversed. As our nation became more thickly populated, as our highway network became surfaced with all-weather roads, smaller stockyards and packing plants have sprung up throughout all the cattle-finishing states, and there are stock trucks to bring the cattle to market and refrigerated trucks to distribute the meat.

But our railroad refrigerator car still does valiant service. It brings fresh apples from Washington or New York, oranges and grapefruit from California or Florida, produce from the garden districts of the nation.

The refrigerator cars—and trucks—have made it possible for Minnesota and Wisconsin to become dairy states. Today, whether you live in California or Maine, you may be putting Wisconsin butter on your toast tomorrow at breakfast. Without some means of transporting butter long distances, there would be no point in Wisconsin's producing more butter than Wisconsin people need. Thus swift transportation makes it possible for certain regions to specialize in the production of goods for which tradition and training have fitted them.

Loading cattle.

Santa Fe Railway

But as your eye runs down the line of rumbling freight cars, you see many other strange types, each designed for a special purpose. There are hopper cars with trap doors in the bottom, filled with coal, gravel, or sand. Some of these hopper cars are tightly covered to protect their loads from the weather. They carry such perishables as cement, lime, potash, bulk livestock feed, and an incredible variety of chemicals. In fact, covered hopper cars have become so useful that the fleet grew in fifteen years from a few hundred to more than fifty thousand.

Ewing Galloway

Filling oil cars at a pipeline.

Some of the hopper-type cars you see may carry bulk flour or sugar. The bottom of this car is covered with a fabric. When the car is unloaded air is forced through the fabric, which slightly lifts the flour or sugar, causing it to flow toward the outlet in the bottom of the car.

You see cylinder-shaped tank cars filled with oil, gasoline, liquid

A special loader with a 217 ton transformer.

Union Pacific Railroad

Union Pacific Railroad

Piggyback cars.

chemicals, molasses, or mineral water. They have valves and faucets at the bottom to draw off the liquid.

There are plain wood boxcars with sliding doors, loaded with canned goods, clothing, furniture, grain; stock cars with slatted sides filled with cattle; double-deck stock cars loaded with sheep or hogs.

You see flatcars loaded with steel beams or huge machines, and very likely you will also see a flatcar on which two highway vans are sitting, their wheels braced and chained, and you wonder why highway semitrailers are riding on a railroad.

This is called the piggyback service. Highway haulers, instead of traveling long distances over the road, simply load their vans or trucks on a railroad flatcar and let the railroad take them to

A crane deposits a loaded van on a flat car.

their destination. At the end of the ride, a truck tractor hooks itself onto the van and delivers its contents to the customer. Many railroads today own and operate truck lines, and use the piggyback system for long hauls, thereby relieving some of the congestion on our highways.

One of the cars you see may be a container car. It consists of a number of separate metal sections each containing a load of goods from a single shipper. At the arrival point, a metal container may be put on a truck and taken direct to the buyer. It is simply an improved way of handling small lots of goods.

That innocent-looking boxcar toward the end of the train may have an unusual interior. Car makers are now producing "damage-free" cars, equipped with rails, crossbars, and movable partitions, so that loads can be held in place and prevented from sliding.

At the end of the freight train is a caboose containing bunks for conductor and brakeman. There is a cupola sticking up from the roof of the caboose with windows on all four sides, through which the brakeman can see what's going on in all directions. Or the caboose may have bay windows to serve the same purpose.

Our own train flies through the country, and faintly through the closed windows we hear the engineer give one long blast on his whistle. He is saying to the conductor: "We are approaching a town."

The conductor reaches for the whistle cord overhead and pulls it three times. We hear three faint hisses of air. The conductor has told the engineer to stop at the town.

Then, from outside, come three separate blasts. The engineer has replied: "Very well, I'll stop."

In case of an emergency the conductor might give two pulls on his whistle cord, meaning, "Stop at once." Or, if the train is standing still, he may give three blasts, meaning, "Back up."

As our train slows down for the stop, we pass a great freight yard

Electronic yards, like this one at Corwith, Illinois, automatically sort thousands of freight cars every day.
Sante Fe Railway

Chief Way

with scores of tracks and switches. Perhaps you wondered, when you saw that hundred-car freight train carrying all types of goods to scores of separate destinations, just how a railroad made sure that each car went to the right town.

The puzzle becomes clearer after we have inspected a freight yard such as the one we are passing. This is an automatic, or "electronic" freight yard.

Think of a freight yard as being divided into three parts: a receiving yard, a classification yard, and a departure yard. Now watch that freight train coming into the receiving yard. A switch engine pushes it along the track and up an artificial hill called a "hump." But before it gets to the hump, as it passes over the track, an electric eye counts it and passes the information to a central tower. Other electronic detectors examine the wheels for broken flanges or dragging equipment, and if faults are found the yard conductor assigns the car to "sick bay" on a repair track. Still farther along, the car is weighed and the information automatically passed to the proper office.

At the top of the hump the first car is uncoupled and coasts down the other side of the hump, pulled by gravity. In the older yards, a brakeman has to accompany every car to brake it down as it approaches its outgoing train. In the automatic yard, no man is needed.

Communications room at East Los Angeles freight house.

Union Pacific Railroad

From the bottom of the hump, classifying tracks fan out in all directions, and, as the descending car rolls down the hump and reaches level ground, its speed is retarded by steel "muscles" that squeeze the wheels. The track the car will take is determined by pushing a button in the control tower, and the retarding is also controlled from there.

There will be other cars on the track ahead of the moving car, and as it approaches the rear of the one directly ahead, another retarder slows it down some more, so that it gently couples itself to the front car, with hardly a jolt.

Cars roll over the hump at the rate of four per minute. You see them rolling sedately along with no man aboard, fanning out one after the other on separate tracks, according to whether they are bound for the adjacent city, a town farther down the line, or a destination in some other direction.

Yards like this occupy from six hundred to eight hundred acres, contain thirty to eighty tracks, and can handle literally thousands of cars per day, sorting them out and speeding them on their way.

In this manner our coal, hats, groceries, television sets, light bulbs, rugs, wallpaper, magazines and books, grain and feed flow in continuous streams to all parts of the nation.

Railroads often carry unusual loads too.

Union Pacific Railroad

Before the days of swift transportation, small hamlets—if they wanted the comforts of life—had to build these comforts for themselves. They cobbled their own shoes, spun their own thread, wove their own rugs, churned their own butter, put up their own meat. A shipment of books or lace or spices or iron tools by pack train or barge was considered a great event in the frontier town.

Communities are no longer self-sufficient. Iowa depends on Connecticut for hats and firearms. Connecticut looks to Iowa for ham and beef. North Dakota depends on Illinois for farm machinery, and Illinois depends on Dakota for wheat. Idaho depends on New England and the Carolinas for textiles, and these areas look to Idaho and Maine for potatoes. A small general store in Wyoming will have on its shelf goods from most of the states of the Union and many foreign countries.

And all this depends on swift and reliable transportation.

Our stainless steel train is now reaching a speed of ninety miles an hour on the plains leading toward Denver, and your mind goes back to the day when Westinghouse saw two trains collide near Schenectady, New York. You wonder how trains are prevented from meeting head-on today.

The system by which moving trains are safeguarded is known as the automatic electric signal block. All our main lines are divided into short sections called "blocks."

At the beginning of each block is a signal with a movable arm called a semaphore.

This arm has three positions. When it is vertical, the engineer knows that the track is clear for two blocks ahead. When the semaphore is in a diagonal position, the block ahead is clear, but the second block has a train in it. When the semaphore is horizontal, the block ahead is occupied and the train must come to a stop, after which it may go ahead slowly.

In addition to the arm position, the signal shows green, yellow, and red lights—green for clear, yellow for caution, and red for stop —just like the automobile traffic signals in your home town.

Union Pacific Railroad

Let's stand by the track a moment and watch a train enter a block. As it approaches, the signal arm is vertical, indicating "all clear." As the train enters the block, the arm swings to a horizontal position. No human hand has operated the signal. It was done by electricity. The signal is wired to the track so that a continuous current is flowing through the block. When the train entered the block it short-circuited the current, causing the signal to change to the stop position, as a warning to the next train to come along.

The train disappears down the track and shortly we see the semaphore arm swing to the diagonal, meaning that the train has entered the second block ahead. After a short wait the arm swings to the vertical. The track is clear for two blocks ahead.

On perhaps one-tenth of the railroad mileage of this country, the chance for human error is reduced to the vanishing point by the "automatic train control." This means that if the engineer ignores a stop signal, the brakes are automatically applied, without any action on his part.

The automatic block is merely one phase of the complicated, smooth-running organization of a railroad. The personnel is as highly organized as the mechanism. The operation of a road is governed by a general manager. The line is divided into divisions of several hundred miles each, varying in length according to the amount of traffic, and each division is headed by a division superintendent.

The division superintendent has two assistants—a trainmaster who has charge of train crews, and a chief dispatcher who issues the orders for the movement of all trains in his division.

The dispatcher has several rules to guide him in moving trains. First, he knows that trains are divided into classes. Fast passenger trains making few stops are first-class; local or accommodation trains are second-class. Freight trains are similarly divided into classes, the express trains having preference over slower freights.

The dispatcher knows also that trains traveling in one direction have superiority over trains of the same class traveling in the other direction.

Dispatching trains is fairly simple when trains live up to their schedules and there are few extra trains. But when, through mechanical trouble or weather conditions, trains become late—or when there are many special trains—the dispatcher is a busy man. In these circumstances his job is to keep all trains out of one another's way, and

Microwave tower.

Union Pacific Railroad

to get them to their destinations as quickly as possible, at the same time observing the rules as to class of trains and direction.

The present organization of the railroad is the result of a hundred years of trial and error. As we lean back in the cushions of our transcontinental flyer and gaze out at the marching panorama of towns and fields, there are thousands of men behind the scenes—dispatchers, mechanics, section hands, superintendents—who are contributing their bit to make our ride swift, safe, and comfortable.

English automobile, 1828.

15 · AUTOMOBILES APPEAR

WHILE railroads were reaching out to new towns, new states, new territories, tying the United States together with bands of steel, inventive men in many parts of the country were struggling toward *something* that was eventually to become the automobile.

We think of the automobile as appearing on the scene in the 1890's, but self-propelled carriages appeared on our roads much earlier than that. Even before Fulton built the *Clermont,* Oliver Evans, the Philadelphia inventor, ran a steam-driven vehicle down the street to the Delaware River. It had wheels and it was boat-shaped, and ran both in water and on land. That was in 1804.

In the years that followed, men came forth with other steam-driven vehicles. Springfield, Massachusetts, saw one in 1825; Vincennes,

Indiana, in the same year; and New York City in 1829. There are pictures of a high-hatted gentleman named Richard Dudgeon driving a steam carriage in New York City in 1860.

It was not until 1893, however, that the fumblings were to take a new turn which was to result in the modern automobile. Beginning in that year, five men in different parts of the country were to produce flimsy horseless carriages, and these carriages were powered with gasoline engines, not steam.

The immediate American pioneers of the automobile were Duryea, Haynes, Winton, Olds, and Ford, and they made their bow in about that order, although to some extent their work overlapped.

It was Charles Duryea, with the help of his brother Frank, who drove the first successful gasoline-powered automobile on the streets of an American town. The memorable year was 1893 and the place Springfield, Massachusetts.

It was just what you would expect the first automobile to be, a light, single-seater buggy with a small motor—four horsepower—under the seat. It steered with a tiller and weighed, engine and all, seven hundred pounds. It may be seen today in the Smithsonian Institution at Washington, D. C. Look at it, when you visit Washington, and make your bow to the grandparent of the millions of cars, busses, and trucks that whizz over our highways and crowd our city streets today.

Charles Duryea in his first Duryea automobile.
Brown Brothers

It couldn't have made much of a stir at the time. No driver's permit was required to run it. No license plates adorned its front and rear buggy axles. Its motor ran with the deliberation of a gasoline pump, every chug distinguishable from every other. When it passed on the street, people glanced at it, rubbed their eyes, and glanced again.

In 1894, Elwood Haynes, employed by the Portland, Indiana, Natural Gas and Oil Company, produced a gasoline car, and four years later was to organize the Haynes Automobile Company and begin to manufacture cars.

The next year, Alexander Winton, a bicycle manufacturer, rambled over the streets of Cleveland in his gasoline buggy. Up in Lansing, Michigan, that year, Ransom Eli Olds was building a gas buggy after having produced two steam-powered carriages.

In the spring of 1896, a tall man wheeled another contraption out of the yard of his house onto Bagley Avenue, in Detroit. It was as funny-looking as the Duryea buggy. It had 28-inch wire bicycle wheels supporting a buggy seat. Under the seat was a two-cylinder engine that generated four horsepower. It had two forward speeds, obtained by shifting a belt from one pulley to another.

The man was Henry Ford, employed as an engineer by the Edison Electric Company at seventy-five dollars a month. He had built the auto in a brick shop in back of his home, and for want of a better name had dubbed it a quadricycle. He had labored months on it and

Henry Ford and his first car.

The Benz Velocipede (1892).

now he was ready to try it out. He chose the nighttime partly because he worked during the day, and partly because fewer people and carriages were abroad at night. He could give it a test without having people look on and laugh if it failed to work. Only his wife, Clara Bryant Ford, knew what was happening.

He cranked the thing, got into the seat, and started up. It ran. He got it back to the house and into the shop and went to bed that night dreaming of the day when he might make a few hundred of the self-propelled buggies and sell them. Today in Detroit, on the front of a modern office building housing an ornate movie palace, you will find a small bronze plaque mentioning the fact that here stood the house in which Henry Ford lived while he was building his first automobile.

These crude experiments were the beginning of the automobile industry in this country. But the United States was several years behind the rest of the world. By 1895, Europe was manufacturing and selling cars and running road races. To Europe must go the credit for creating the automobile.

For several decades before 1890, French, English, and German inventors had been experimenting with engines that burned first illu-

The European Daimler Victoria (1894).

minating gas, then vaporized oil, then vaporized gasoline. These early engines were heavy and slow, but in the 1880's a German named Gottlieb Daimler designed a lighter, faster engine that would revolve 800 times a minute instead of the former 150.

In 1886, Daimler put one of these engines into a carriage, and another German, Charles Benz, put one into a tricycle.

Then a Frenchman named Levassor, of the Panhard-Levassor Company in Paris, designed a car that looked more like automobiles as we know them. It had the engine under a hood in front of the car and a clutch and sliding-gear transmission to carry the power to the rear wheels. In 1892 he began manufacturing the car. By 1895, while Americans were still experimenting with home-built gas buggies, Benzes, Daimlers, and Panhard-Levassors were well known in Europe, and a few had been imported into this country.

Thus Europe created and developed the motor car. The very name, "automobile," is French. But America, once she decided to accept the new invention, entered into its manufacture with typical American speed and optimism. And the man who first produced autos in quantity was Ransom Eli Olds.

Most builders at the beginning of the twentieth century were producing a few cars at high price. Olds decided to build many cars at low price. With the help of financial backers, he incorporated the Olds Motor Works in 1899 and built a factory on the river bank in Detroit. For a while he built and sold stationary gasoline engines, but in 1901 he produced a car called the "curved-dash" Oldsmobile.

It wasn't much more impressive than the early experiments of the pioneers. It had wire wheels, a buggy seat, and an engine under the floor. But it suited the customer well. It weighed only seven hundred pounds and cost first $600, then $650. It was simply constructed, easy to operate, and easy to repair. That very first year Olds built and sold 425 cars.

At the same time, a young employee of Mr. Olds, Roy Chapin, drove one of the curved-dash cars across country to New York, to display it at the automobile show. It was a venturesome drive for that day. Through New York state the roads were so bad that Chapin had to take to the towpath of the Erie Canal, thereby incurring the rage of canal-boat drivers who didn't want their mules frightened. The Oldsmobile aroused excitement at the show and sales boomed.

The next year the Olds factory built 2,500 curved-dash cars; the following year 4,000; and in 1904, 5,000. Today a single company can produce 5,000 cars in a day, but for those days 5,000 was a sensational year's production.

Ransom Olds had proved that if cars were made well and cheaply, the demand would exceed the supply. Unfortunately, his stockholders decided that there was more money in expensive cars. Olds disagreed

The curved-dash Oldsmobile.

The Stanley brothers in their steam car.
Brown Brothers

and finally sold out, leaving the cheap car field to the man who had run his home-made car down Bagley Avenue one April night in 1896.

This man, Henry Ford, had already organized two companies with no great success. He had been feeling his way along, building both expensive and low-cost cars. In 1903 he organized his third company, the Ford Motor Company. He produced a two-cylinder car retailing from $850 up, buying the engines from the Dodge Brothers, makers of stationary engines; buying his bodies, springs, and wheels elsewhere; and assembling the parts in his small plant. He sold 1,708 cars that first year.

During the next few years he continued to experiment with cars of varying prices and always found that as the price went up, sales dropped. Finally, in 1907–8, he decided to concentrate upon the cheap car. He designed runabouts ranging in price from $600 to $750 and at once his sales jumped to 8,423.

In the autumn of 1908 he produced, for the first time, his famous Model T, a car so simply built that almost anyone could repair it, so light and inexpensive that almost anyone could buy and run it. From that time on, for many years, Fords outnumbered all other cars on the highways.

Meanwhile, in these early years, an interesting battle went on between three types of cars—gasoline, electric, and steam. It was by no means certain, at the beginning of the century, that the cars of the future would be gasoline cars.

Out for a spin around Central Park, New York, in an electric car.
Brown Brothers

Stanley and White steamers were a common sight on our streets. They ran with a smooth, hissing sound, and nobody knew just how fast they would go. Prizes were offered to men who would open the throttle and keep it open, regardless of how fast the car went. Nobody ever dared accept the challenge.

There were many electric cars, too, gliding about the streets as silently as ghosts. They were extremely easy to handle and popular with ladies because it was not necessary to crank them.

But steam and electric cars had faults that the gasoline car did not have. Steam cars carried tanks of water that must be heated before the car could start. When you went out to your car in the morning, you had to wait until the steam pressure was up before you could go anywhere. And now and then a tank exploded.

The trouble with the electric car was its limited range. You could run it only so many miles before you had to recharge the batteries—and it took many hours to get the batteries charged.

The gasoline car would start with the turn of a crank—some of the time—and you could be on your way instantly instead of waiting until steam pressure rose. As contrasted with the electric car, its range was unlimited. All you had to do was refill your gas tank and start off again. And so, as the highways became more and more crowded, steamers and electrics disappeared and the gas car ruled the field.

In those days automobiles were used only when the weather was good. All cars were open. Many of them didn't even have tops. The cars were put up for the winter in the barn and not brought forth until spring.

Since cars were not run in the winter, neither were they sold then. The factories closed their doors late in the fall, not to resume operations until early spring. The auto was a summer plaything.

Automobile owning and driving was not entirely a joy in the first ten years of the century. There was no self-starter and no foot throttle. Wheels were large and bodies high off the ground. Springs were none too good.

Spark and throttle levers were mounted on the steering post, and before you started the car, you had to retard the spark lever, so that when you turned the crank the engine wouldn't backfire and break your arm. If your engine wasn't in tune, you might have to spin the crank to the exhaustion point before a few sputtering barks told you that the engine had finally caught hold. Then you ran to the front seat to advance the spark before the engine stalled.

Once under way, you adjusted the speed of the engine with a hand throttle. Because of the high-pressure tires and hard springs you slowed down for every bump, and in those days the bumps were frequent.

If you were going into the country you soon came to gravel, and on dry days the passage of every auto was marked by a trailing cloud of dust. Before long you ran off the gravel onto plain dirt, and here a brown cloud of dust replaced the white cloud. No wonder automobilists wore linen dusters, caps, and goggles.

Some of these dirt roads were improved by the simple process of dumping stone over them and letting the traffic pack the stone into a surface. Rather than cut your tires to pieces on the jagged edges of the stone, you would carefully steer your auto into the wagon track that ran parallel to the road. This usually consisted of two dirt tracks with a ridge of turf between. On this trail you could often get your speed up to twenty-five miles an hour, which was considered fast for

Culver Pictures, Inc.

Changing a tire.

country driving. If you could maintain an average of fifteen miles per hour on a hundred-mile cross-country trip, you could congratulate yourself.

It was no fun changing tires in those days. Tires were inflated to seventy pounds pressure and seldom lasted more than 1,500 miles. When a bang or the whistle of escaping air warned you of a flat, you had to stop, jack up the wheel, and pry off the tire with a set of flat tire tools. Then you laid the tire on a grassy plot and pulled out the inner tube, to look for the puncture.

You either repaired the inner tube with a rubber patch and some glue, or put a new tube into the casing. Then it was another burdensome job to work the tire back onto the wheel, after which you dragged out the pump and bent over the handle for a quarter-hour of backbreaking toil. The man who could take off and patch a tire in an hour was unusually skillful.

Considering the muscle work involved in starting cars and repairing tires, it is no wonder that few women drove autos. Until the self-starter invented by C. F. Kettering was placed on a Cadillac car in 1912, woman drivers were rare. And only after the improvement in rubber manufacture produced a tire that would go thousands of miles without a puncture was the woman driver a common sight.

But while Ford, Olds, Winton, Studebaker, Duryea, and other early manufacturers were putting the world on wheels, the roads were not much better than the trails our forefathers had traveled a hundred years before. In 1900, 8,000 cars were registered in this country. By 1905 the number had increased to 77,400, and these pioneer drivers set up a roar of protest over the condition of our highways.

In reality, the automobilists merely added their voices to a protest that was already making itself felt. In 1900 there were ten million bicycles in this country. The nation was enjoying a bicycle craze. The popular song of the day was "Bicycle Built for Two." Every town of any size had its bicycle race track. The most famous man in any town was the one who had ridden a hundred miles in one day. This feat earned him a Century award and put him in a class apart.

Bicycle fever.

A cartoon of the 1800's

The League of American Wheelmen, millions strong, was agitating for better roads. The members had formed a national organization and loosed a barrage of petitions, speeches, and stories in the papers and magazines. The campaign was under way when motorists joined it with a will.

Since improved highways were so important to the growing automobile industry, it might be well to make a quick review of the history of highways in the United States.

The first road in New England was established in 1639 between Boston and Plymouth. This road and all other roads of the period were merely trails worn down by wagon wheels. Out of Boston a trail reached out toward Connecticut because New Englanders had heard about the wonderful land to be occupied in the valley of the Connecticut River and wished to migrate there. Gradually Boston, New York, and Philadelphia became connected by roads over which only a horse and rider could travel.

Then, in the generation before the Revolution, came the stage lines and our first good-roads agitation. Trails that became bottomless lanes of mud in wet weather would not do. Drivers and travelers demanded stone surfaces.

In 1800 Pennsylvania recognized the pressing need for highways by fostering turnpikes—improved stone roads built by private companies which charged tolls. By 1828 Pennsylvania had 3,110 miles of chartered turnpike costing $8,000,000, and other states were following her example.

During this turnpike activity, America learned from England how to build a macadam surface. We have already seen how the federal government built its splendid macadam highway, thirty feet wide, from Cumberland on the Potomac, to Wheeling on the Ohio. In the early years of the nineteenth century, both the federal government and the states were engaged in strenuous highway building.

Why did not the United States continue this good work? Why did not we provide ourselves with a widespread network of hard-surfaced roadways like those in Europe? Europe's rulers had built roads for

Culver Pictures, Inc.

What the pioneer automobilist had to put up with.

two main purposes—war and commerce. The Caesars and Napoleons of the Old World had constructed highways over which they could quickly move their troops, in order to maintain control over conquered lands. The cities of Europe were centuries old. Ordinary trade and migration between them had required good roads long before America had even been discovered. And all this road building had been completed before the railroad was dreamed of.

The United States had barely made her start on highways when Peter Cooper, Horatio Allen, and Phineas Davis were running their baby locomotives over tracks of strap iron in Baltimore and Charleston. It was much easier to connect towns with tracks of wood and iron than it was to build highways. Easier, cheaper, and more exciting. It was faster, too, riding in a railroad coach at twenty-five miles an hour than in a stagecoach at ten.

We have already seen how rapidly the railroad conquered space in this country. It is no wonder, then, that turnpikes were abandoned, stone surfaces fell into disrepair, and good roads ceased to be. When the automobile came to Europe, it had beautiful roads over which to run. When the auto came to America, it got stuck in the mud.

At the advent of the automobile, road maintenance—such as it was—was still the responsibility of the township. Supervisors who knew very little about roads were in charge. Property owners could either pay their road tax in money, or work out the tax on the highway.

In 1891 New Jersey improved on this system a bit by providing state aid and laying out a state network of highways. Other states followed suit.

The next step was taken by the United States government in response to the agitation of the bicyclists. In 1893 Congress appropriated $10,000 and created the Office of Public Roads Inquiries. Qualified experts went around the country showing township and state officials how to build roads.

Then, in 1904, the United States made a census of roads in this country. How many miles of road did we have, anyhow? The census revealed that we had a total of 2,151,570 miles, of which only a few insignificant miles were dustless.

By 1915 there were 2,309,666 registered automobiles in the country, and the government decided to become the partner of the states in road building. The following year Congress provided federal aid for rural post roads and appropriated $5,000,000. In the next four years it added $270,000,000 more, distributing its generosity over the country in proportion to the population and the amount of rural

Country road, 1904.

Brown Brothers

Brown Brothers

The sign tells how to "preserve our roads." The license plate reads "1913."

roads in each state. On all federal aid roads, the government contributed half the cost.

In 1921 the Federal Highway Act was passed and our system of national and state roads came into existence. Hereafter, under the supervision of the government, states would build roads with a view to creating a comprehensive national network. Under the supervision of the state highway departments, localities within the state would improve roads with a view to creating state networks. State and national networks would combine into a general system. Meanwhile, technical schools and highway departments would experiment with concrete, macadam, gravel, and other surfaces and learn the best way to build them. With a will, the United States went to work building roads.

The first road census had revealed that the United States had a little over two million miles of road, practically all of it unfit for automobile travel. Today, there are more than 3,400,000 miles of road, of which 400,000 are city streets. Of the three million or so miles of rural roads, about one million are still dirt. The other two million are surfaced with gravel or something better, and no less than

Getting a ticket, 1913.

Culver Pictures, Inc.

one-half million miles have high-type surfaces such as blacktop and cement.

There has been no highway-building program like this anywhere in the world, and the program has cost great sums of money. The Bureau of Public Roads in Washington estimates that an ordinary tar-treated gravel road in a rural area costs fifty thousand dollars a mile, not counting the cost of the right of way. Those high-speed four-lane divided highways, on the other hand, average a half-million dollars per mile in rural areas and no less than four million dollars per mile (average) in the cities! During the mid-1950's alone, our state, federal, and county governments were spending well over six billion dollars a year on our highways.

Where does the money come from? In 1920, most of our highway money was raised by bond issues financed by property taxes, but as the demand for better highways grew, the burden on the property holder was too great.

In 1919, the state of Oregon pointed the way by levying the first gasoline tax in history, and in succeeding years every state—and even the federal government—passed gasoline taxes. A gas tax is called a "user" tax, because the user of the highway pays as he drives. Every time he fills his tank, he pays taxes to the state and federal governments.

Today the car driver pays out a goodly sum of money in user taxes. In addition to gas taxes, he pays for license plates, drivers' licenses, and federal taxes (known as excise taxes) on various automotive parts. He pays tolls on ferries, bridges, and turnpikes. These sums approximate six billion dollars a year. Thus it seems that the automobile driver is doing a good job of footing the bill for our highways.

It is an interesting repetition of history that in the mid-twentieth century our country again engaged in a fever of turnpike building, as it did early in the 1800's. Pennsylvania was a leader in that first turnpike era, and Pennsylvania was also a leader in the modern turnpike development.

In July, 1940, the Keystone State opened the first 160 miles of the famed Pennsylvania Turnpike—from Harrisburg to Pittsburgh. This swift stretch of dual highway, boring through hills in long tunnels and sweeping in graceful curves through the Allegheny Mountains, captured the imagination of people and was a financial success from the start. People didn't mind at all paying approximately a cent a mile to ride on it.

Other states followed Pennsylvania's lead—New Jersey, Ohio, Indiana, New York, Oklahoma, Kansas, Colorado. In 1958, there were over three thousand miles of turnpike, on which drivers paid tolls averaging something over a cent a mile. The New York State Thruway is 497 miles long, following closely the route of the Erie Canal from Buffalo to Albany and from there paralleling the path of Fulton's *Clermont* down to New York City. Indiana, Ohio, and Pennsylvania built their turnpikes end to end, so that it is possible to drive from Chicago to Philadelphia or New York without ever getting off the limited-access highway.

Culver Pictures, Inc.

Beginning in 1956, however, the federal government authorized a program of superhighway construction that spelled the end of any further turnpike building. Federal and state authorities outlined a system of highways forty-one thousand miles long, connecting all our principal centers of population. This nationwide network goes by the name of the National System of Interstate and Defense Highways, or, more briefly, the Interstate System.

Practically all of this great mileage will be of the limited-access kind, just as the turnpikes are. Most of it will have two lanes each way, with a median strip in the middle. There will be no grade crossings. These highways, almost long enough to go twice around the world, will soar over railroads and rivers, tunnel through hills, and pass over or under opposing streets. The only difference between these highways and the turnpikes is that the Interstate System will be free. On this system the federal government will pay ninety cents out of each dollar spent, the states paying the rest.

Much of the system is already completed or under construction. The rest is scheduled for completion by 1975 at a total cost of approximately thirty-five billion dollars.

At the beginning of the 1960's seventy-six million motor vehicles were registered in this country, over twelve and one-half million of them trucks and buses. Nobody dares predict how high the total will go.

Culver Pictures, Inc.

16 · TRUCKS, BUSES, AND CARS TAKE TO THE ROAD

FOR THE first few years of its life, the automobile was considered a plaything and riding in an automobile a sport, like yachting. It was not long, however, before businessmen began to wonder whether cars could not be used to carry something besides men and women in dusters and goggles.

A few merchants bought passenger cars and converted them into delivery trucks by having carpenters build special bodies for them. For a while, all trucks used in this country were converted passenger cars.

Then manufacturers realized that if cars were to be used for delivering heavy loads, the chassis must be stronger and larger, the engine more powerful. The manufacture of trucks began.

It is not certain just where the use of trucks started, but the chances are that it happened in many places. Trucks, we're told, rolled on Denver streets around the turn of the century. A few years later, a St. Louis newspaper bought fourteen motor delivery wagons (complete with storm curtains and all operating levers inside the curtains!) to replace fifty horse-drawn vehicles. Boston found that it could deliver express to the suburbs at $4.50 per day per truck; venturesome city fathers risked public disapproval by appropriating good tax money for motor-driven fire equipment. Out in the rural areas, farmers were stripping off the bodies of their old cars and building boxes for hauling grain, fruit, and even livestock.

For a time trucks were used only for deliveries in cities. But here

Mail truck, 1913.

Goodyear Tire and Rubber Co.

and there, as early as 1907, men with trucks offered to carry goods between near-by cities, and thus intercity trucking was born. Around the larger towns, trucks were used to carry farm goods to market.

The advantages of the truck were apparent from the start. A farmer located twenty miles from town could ship his load of apples by train, but to do this he would have to haul the apples to the station in his wagon. There they must be transferred to the train. At the city they must be unloaded from the train and carted to the buyer. The truck, on the other hand, could go straight to the farmer's barn, load the apples, and carry them directly to the city market. By truck the number of handlings was reduced from four to two, and usually the truck was a bit cheaper than the railroad.

Until World War I, the use of trucks was confined to towns and short intercity lines. Long-haul trucking was unheard of. The roads were too bad.

But during World War I, conditions made long-haul trucking necessary, no matter what the state of the roads. The war put a strain upon railroads which was greater than the railroads could bear. It was necessary to move people and goods from city to camp and from camp to port. Lumber and supplies must be transported to campsites; farm products had to be carried to the seaboard for shipment to our growing expeditionary force. Efficient as our railroads were, they found themselves unable to do all that was demanded of them. Freight houses became so congested that trains had to dump their bales and boxes along the tracks outside of the city.

How, then, could our goods be carried if trains were overloaded? The answer was the truck. President Wilson appointed a highway Transport Committee and put the Detroit automobile man, Roy Chapin, in charge.

Chapin knew that the government had ordered some thirty thousand trucks for delivery to France, where trucks were all-important in distributing food, clothing, and ammunition to troops. Ordinarily these trucks would have been loaded on railroad flatcars and shipped to the Atlantic Coast.

Troop trucks, 1919.

Culver Pictures, Inc.

Instead of that, Chapin had them driven across country to New York, Boston, Philadelphia, and other ports. Nor did they go empty. They were loaded with clothes, guns, helmets, and other war supplies. These trucks, lurching over bad rural roads to the Atlantic, demonstrated on a large scale the practicability of long-haul trucking.

One of the first companies to take advantage of trucks on a regular schedule was the Goodyear Tire and Rubber Company of Akron, Ohio. During the war they established a route between Akron and

Goodyear Tire and Rubber Co.

Boston 740 miles long and ran seven trucks regularly over it. Instead of going the direct route through New York state, where the bridges were too flimsy for heavy trucks, they went through Pennsylvania to New York City and up the coast.

The Goodyear Company had two reasons for establishing the route. They wished to test their big pneumatic tires by giving them actual road service—at that time most trucks were using solid tires—and they wished to deliver tires to eastern dealers.

Within a year, these big trucks were making the trip each way in four days and giving regular service. Here was a practical demonstration of long-haul trucking.

In view of these developments, it is not strange that our country quickly adopted trucks. In 1915 there were only 158,000 trucks in

Transcontinental truck, 1920.

Parade of trucks, 1919.

Firestone Tire and Rubber Co.

the country. Five years later, the war over, there were a million. In 1960 there were more than 12,000,000.

The years immediately after World War I marked the rise of the great trucking companies, and in practically all cases these companies had small beginnings:

In 1922, two Vermont brothers bought a truck and hauled a load of Vermont butter to Boston, then returned to Vermont with a load of packaged groceries. Today they own hundreds of trucks, tractors and trailers and do a business of several million dollars a year.

In Chicago at about the same time, an ice and coal dealer acquired an extra truck and contracted to carry a cargo of merchandise all the way to Milwaukee. Out in Montana, a man and his wife debated what to do with their savings, then bought a truck. An ex-soldier in

Vegetable trucks, 1920.

Culver Pictures Inc.

Dairy truck, 1958.

Virginia, out of a job, invested his five-hundred-dollar bonus in a secondhand truck and rolled out onto the highway, looking for something to haul. Today, all these beginners are conducting large trucking lines over many states.

Two general types of intercity trucking are now carried on. Fleets of trucks are maintained by private companies to carry their own goods. And there are the for-hire carriers who, like the railroads, will carry anybody's goods for a fee.

Among the private fleets are the great tank trucks belonging to the large oil companies, delivering gasoline and oil to service stations. There are the large dairy companies delivering butter, cheese, and milk to retail stores, and collecting milk from farmers. You have seen their oval tank trucks rumbling over the highways. Packing companies have fleets of refrigerated trucks to carry their dressed meats all over the country. Chain-store systems use trucks to restock their stores.

Other large fleets of company-owned trucks are used for service and repair. The telephone and telegraph company has a fleet of fifty thousand trucks, the largest single fleet in the country, to install phones, repair storm damage, dig postholes, and the like.

Another large fleet of government-owned trucks carries our mail, and you may see on the highway a huge van that is actually a traveling post office. Inside it, clerks are sorting out mail while the truck is going from town to town. Approximately twenty-five thousand cities in the United States receive all their mail by truck.

Among the for-hire trucks are the freight haulers and the movers, whose huge tractor-trailer combinations are a common sight on our highways. There are over a million of these for-hire trucks in the

Ewing Galloway

This van can hold enough furniture for a mansion.

country, more than half of them in intercity service, and they carry 17 per cent of the total commercial hauling job in the United States.

Trucks have become especially useful for carrying certain kinds of goods. An aluminum furniture van will back up to your front door and swallow within its padded sides all the furniture and goods of a ten-room house, and you can leave the packing to the driver. Your clothing goes directly from your closets into wardrobe boxes. Your rugs are rolled and hung in straps, your dishes packed in barrels, your mattresses slipped into paper cartons to prevent soiling. The big doors of the van, fitted like refrigerator doors, keep out all dust and moisture.

Although van rates are higher than freight rates, vans save much packing and handling, and they take your goods directly from your old home to your new. There are over four thousand carriers licensed to haul household goods, and they do practically all the moving that is done in this country.

In transporting livestock from farm to market, trucks have replaced railroads as the chief means of transport. Where in 1916 less than 2 per cent of all livestock was transported by truck, by 1958 four-fifths of all livestock was riding the highway to market. And each year the percentage increases.

Many special trucking operations have developed over the years. Large vans that are in reality traveling refrigerators carry fresh fruits and vegetables from California's Imperial Valley, from Florida, and from the Rio Grande to the city markets of the nation. Out of Morgan

City, Louisiana, and Jacksonville, Florida, other refrigerated trucks fan out to northern markets with shrimp, mackerel, pompano, crabmeat, and sea trout. From Florida and Louisiana markets, great loads of strawberries go north to city markets and large ice-cream plants.

A good way to measure the importance of the truck to American life is to stand on the street corner of a small town on any weekday. In one day, from twenty to thirty trucks will come into town. You will see a soft-drink truck backing up to the local soda bar; a meat truck bringing sides of beef and pork to the local butcher; a big van carrying hardware from a city a hundred miles away; bread trucks unloading large baskets of bread from a city bakery that services thousands of stores and restaurants in half the state; ice-cream trucks, cigarette trucks, chain-store vans, large tandem transports with gasoline for the local bulk tanks; big flat-bed trucks bringing steel to the local factory; a swift pickup delivering the big-city daily paper; a bookmobile bringing books to the village library; and a traveling tuberculosis laboratory giving free examinations to anyone in the town who wants one.

The truck and the highway have tied all small towns within a thirty-mile circle into one loosely knit community. The dry cleaner, laundryman, dairyman, and repairman even serve the farms of the countryside on a house-to-house basis, thus making the farmer a part of the community.

Over fifty thousand communities in the United States are served

American Library Association

only by truck. Without daily truck deliveries, these towns would soon be without the goods and services necessary to sustain present-day life.

There are trucks that you and I seldom see. These are the rugged workhorses that do their jobs off the highway, in mines, lumber camps, and oil fields. In the Minnesota iron mines are dump trucks with a capacity of eighteen tons, plus a few monsters of forty tons. To bring uranium ore out of the Rockies, huge three-axle dump trucks operate at altitudes of thirteen thousand feet, up 30 per cent grades, over trails called "impassable."

In the oil fields are trucks carrying portable drilling rigs with derricks that go fifty feet into the air when extended, and small enclosed trucks that are in reality traveling electrical laboratories, capable of giving technicians an accurate picture of rock formations thousands of feet under ground.

Trucks now haul most of the nation's timber from forest to lumber mill, and in the West, where the trees run large, these timber haulers have anywhere from sixteen to twenty wheels.

Trucks have become big business. There are more than 6,500,000 truck drivers in the United States. More than 7,200,000 people are engaged in truck transportation, or almost one out of every ten people employed in the nation.

Over the past forty years, motor buses have steadily grown to a position of importance in the transportation of passengers and small freight between cities.

One of the true ancestors of this big business is the "jitney." To visualize how the "jitney" came into being, imagine yourself the owner of a passenger car. You wish to make a little money, so you put a sign on the side of your car saying, "Mack Avenue via Fourth," then halt your car at some busy street corner and get a load of passengers who wish to go to Mack Avenue.

Thousands of private car owners did exactly that shortly before

Jitney bus, 1915.
Ewing Galloway

and during World War I. The drivers usually charged five cents for a ride and "jitney" was slang for five cents. Hence the cars were called "jitneys."

Jitneys had several advantages over streetcars. They could go anywhere. They could serve a new subdivision without waiting for

OUR OVERCROWDED STREET-CARS.
"Plenty of room!" shout the Conductors. "Take your chances and swell our dividends," insolently demand half-a-dozen Railway Monopolists. But the People, stupidly patient as they have been, are beginning to ask when the Legislature will decree, "NO SEAT, NO FARE!"

Bus, 1920.

tracks to be built. They could load passengers at the curb instead of compelling them to walk out to the middle of the street. They were more quiet.

It wasn't long before some car owners were offering rides to near-by towns. One of these men was Carl Eric Wickman, who began carrying passengers between Hibbing, Minnesota, and Alice, in 1914, charging fifteen cents one way and twenty-five cents a round trip. To accommodate more passengers, he built large bodies and put them on trucks.

By 1917 he had opened lines to several towns and was earning forty thousand dollars a year. As business grew better, he and his partners bought other short lines and connected them, thus extending the range of his operations. Consolidations and mergers followed until this small Minnesota company became the largest bus line in the country, able to take passengers almost anywhere in the United States.

Bus lines did more than reach communities not already served by railroad and the electric interurban lines. They soon proved themselves so economical that they ran most interurban lines out of business. A few interurban lines, reading the handwriting on the wall, bought fleets of buses and let their tracks rust.

Bus, 1922.
Goodyear Tire and Rubber Co.

Railroads, too, began replacing their short feeder lines with buses. They saw no sense in operating even a short train at a cost of ninety cents a mile when buses could provide the same service at twenty cents a mile. In the past generation, the amount of railroad trackage in this country has decreased because of the competition of the highway with its fleets of buses, trucks, and private cars.

The latest heavy buses are worth a short description. The thirty-eight passengers sit in upholstered armchairs that may be tilted to several positions. The floor is higher than the wheels, so that passengers may look over the roofs of passing private cars. There are double-deck buses, too, seating forty-three passengers. The upper passengers sit in a kind of greenhouse with a windshield in front, where they get a fine view of the passing sights.

Nearly all intercity buses, these days, are air-conditioned, and some have toilets and washrooms. Luggage is stored underneath the floor in weathertight compartments, and there are racks inside for hand luggage.

You can depart from the handsome Chicago bus terminal an hour after midnight, on Monday, and after two and one-half days spent in rolling across plains and over mountains, arrive in Los Angeles early on Wednesday. Every few hours your bus will stop for meals and leg-stretching at an Iowa county seat, a western cow town, or a mountain village. Traveling by bus you not only travel at low cost,

but you also have a chance to rub elbows with your neighbors in the average American town.

The rise of the motor bus as an intercity passenger carrier has been paralleled by the rise of the school bus in the transportation of children. In 1919, only a handful of students traveled to school by bus. In a recent year, over twelve million pupils were picked up at street corners and rural stops by more than 160,000 buses and delivered to the school door.

The highway, the school bus, and the private automobiles of parents have made great changes in our school system. In pioneer days, the only way rural children could be given an education was to build a one-room schoolhouse out in the country. Here, one teacher attempted to teach six or eight grades to a roomful of pupils, all at one time. The school had to be within walking distance of the farm families it served, and "walking distance" often meant two or three miles. At one time there were over 200,000 one-room schools in the United States.

Then, as highways improved and even the secondary rural roads were improved and maintained, rural school districts got together and consolidated into single schools in the nearest village. One-room schools began to disappear from the scene. By 1939, the number had dropped to 113,600, and by 1953 to less than 50,000! And at last report they were still disappearing at the rate of a half-dozen a day.

While the truck, the intercity bus, and the school bus have all done their share in changing our way of living, the role played by the millions of passenger cars owned by Americans, rich and poor, must not be overlooked.

Many of our young people today have never ridden on a train, an airplane, or even a de luxe motor bus. When they go on hunting and fishing trips, or family vacations, they go by car. When they go to college their parents take them in the automobile. When they go job-hunting in a near-by city they borrow the family "bus." With their first dollars, they make a down payment on a secondhand car and join the hordes on the road.

No less than 88 per cent of all intercity travel is by car, leaving

Culver Pictures, Inc.

Trucks in World War II.

only 12 per cent to be divided up by the railroads, buses, airplanes, and waterways. The ability of the average citizen to get into his automobile, step on the starter, and travel anywhere he pleases, for business, pleasure, or emergency, has created a freedom of travel never before realized in the history of the world.

All this has vastly changed the face of the United States. Motels, drive-in theaters, drive-in restaurants, large suburban shopping centers with spacious parking lots, roadside stands selling everything from straw hats to fruit to angleworms to pottery to weather vanes . . . these are a familiar part of our highway scene.

Because of the automobile and the highway, our national and state parks are jammed with visitors on every sunny vacation day. Our cities have sprawled out into the surrounding countryside, and our wage earners travel many miles to work. The village store has gradually given way to the larger store in the county seat, because people don't mind traveling eight or ten miles to shop. Our open-country schools and churches are giving way to schools and churches in town. Our great-grandfathers would hardly know the United States, if they were to see it today.

Brown Brothers

The flight at Kitty Hawk. Orville Wright is lying down on the wing. Wilbur Wright is on the ground.

17 · TWO AMERICANS TAKE WING

On a freezing December morning in 1903, several men stood beside a strange-looking device on the side of a sandy hill at Kitty Hawk, North Carolina.

Two of the men were brothers, Wilbur and Orville Wright, and the device was a biplane. Its two wings were about thirty feet long and four feet wide, and the surfaces were slightly curved. The wings were braced by light wood, bamboo, and wire, and a 139-pound engine was attached to the lower wing near the center of its span. It was a gasoline engine developing twelve horsepower.

Instead of landing wheels there were sledlike skids under the lower wing, and the craft rested on a greased wooden rail sixty feet long. With men at either wing tip to balance the plane, it was expected that the craft would slide down the rail and take off from the ground.

The few onlookers from the near-by lifesaving station had never seen anything like this ship before. Nobody in the world had. They couldn't have, because nothing exactly like it had ever been built before.

The engine was started and Orville lay flat on the lower wing, his hands on the controls that enabled him to manipulate the flexible wing tips and rudder. He was excited. He hadn't been able to sleep the night before. He knew how it felt to soar through the air because he had flown a glider, but he didn't know what it was like to fly a powered machine. Nobody had ever done that in all history, although some had tried.

When the engine was warmed up, a wire holding the ship to the rail was released and the plane started down the greased rail with Wilbur at a wing tip. In forty feet it rose from the rail to a height of ten feet, dipped downward and rose again. About a hundred and twenty feet from the starting point it dipped again, a wing tip struck the ground, and the plane came safely to rest. This was the world's first successful airplane flight.

Man has always wanted to fly because man has always envied the birds. In Greek mythology there is the story of Daedalus, who escaped from the island of Crete by building wings out of wax and feathers, for himself and his son Icarus. Icarus, so the legend runs, flew so near the sun that the heat melted the wax from his wings, causing him to drop into the sea and drown.

From a woodcut, 1493

Down through the centuries, men have speculated on flying, made drawings, and constructed models. As early as the thirteenth century, the famous scientist and philosopher Roger Bacon predicted balloon flights in "a hollow globe filled with etherial air and launched from an elevation into the air, where it will float." Bacon thought of air as a fluid—the very same concept that is held by science today.

In the fifteenth century, the great artist and engineer Leonardo da Vinci built a model helicopter—a wing with a horizontal propeller—and successfully flew it. In his sketches are found drawings of an ornithopter—a pair of flapping wings with which a man might beat the air like a bird.

It was not, however, by heavier-than-air machines but by balloons that man was to achieve his first flight, and the year of this event was 1783, six years before Washington was to be inaugurated President of the United States. In that year, Jacques and Joseph Montgolfier constructed large balloons of paper and silk, built a fire beneath the opening in the bottom of the balloon, thus heating the air inside and making it lighter than the surrounding air. One of their heated-air balloons rose to an estimated height of three thousand feet.

The first man actually to go aloft in a balloon was a young Frenchman named Jean François Pilâtre de Rozier. On October 15, 1783, he climbed into the wicker gallery of a Montgolfier hot-air balloon, a linen bag seventy-four feet in diameter. In the middle of the gallery was a crate with a supply of fuel near-by. By judiciously feeding fuel to the fire, he floated over the roofs of Paris, much to the awe of his earthbound watchers.

Meanwhile, Professor J. A. C. Charles of the *Académie des Sciences* in Paris was experimenting with hydrogen-filled balloons. He built an experimental balloon, thirteen feet in diameter, that drifted from Paris to Gonesse, fifteen miles away. There the startled inhabitants discovered it rolling and bouncing over the ground and decided that it was a living monster. One bold peasant shot it with a gun, and as the balloon started to deflate, the others rushed in with pitchforks and finished it.

Then, in December, 1783, Professor Charles ascended in a larger hydrogen balloon and flew from the Tuileries Gardens in Paris to Nesle, twenty-seven miles away.

The first conquest of the air, then, must go to the balloon, but, while the balloon was becoming an attraction at carnivals, experiments with heavier-than-air machines went on.

Sir George Cayley of England directed thinking along the right channel when he proposed fixed wings—not flapping wings—driven through the air by mechanical power. To demonstrate his theory, he built and successfully flew a fixed-wing glider for a short distance.

In 1848, John Stringfellow worked on a fixed-wing plane driven by steam, but the engines of that day were too heavy for flight. He did, however, successfully launch a small steam-driven model.

In the years that followed, other men came forward to make con-

tributions to the theory of aviation. Alphonse Penaud proposed, in drawings and papers, that the trailing edge of the wing be made movable, so that the airplane could be directed up and down. He proposed a rudder and elevator, both of which are used today, and a wing with a curved surface.

The curved-surface wing was carried further along by Horatio Phillips in 1884. Wind tunnel experiments had shown him that a curved upper surface, deflecting the air current upward, would reduce pressure along the trailing edge of the wing, and this would tend to pull the ship upward.

So, bit by bit, thoughtful men in all parts of the world made their contributions to the idea of flight, and more and more they came to believe that flight could be achieved by a pair of fixed wings with curved surfaces and movable controls to direct the wings in flight. Then came two great experimenters, Otto Lilienthal of Germany and Octave Chanute of the United States, who built these controllable wings, climbed to the tops of hills, and launched themselves into the air to soar and flutter long distances over the invisible currents. Best of all, they made careful notes of the type of craft that would soar best, and it was these notes that the Wrights studied when they built their first gliders.

Otto Lilienthal making a glider flight in 1896.
Brown Brothers

Undoubtedly, if there had been a satisfactory engine, Lilienthal or Chanute would have built a successful powered airplane. But in the nineties, when these men were experimenting, the gasoline engine was still too heavy for its power to pull a plane through the air. So these two courageous men had to join the long roll of advance experimenters who laid the groundwork. A score of daring minds had set the stage for that memorable day at Kitty Hawk, in 1903.

The Wrights themselves deserve a place among the advance experimenters, for before Kitty Hawk they had worked on flight for seven years. During that time they had experimented with models in their Dayton, Ohio, bicycle shop, built and flown gliders, pored over drawings and notes, and finally constructed a lightweight gasoline engine that they thought would pull a pair of wings through the air.

While the Wrights were thus engaged, another American inventor was to come forth and hold the center of the stage for a short time. Samuel Pierpont Langley, secretary of the Smithsonian Institution, had flown a steam-driven model plane successfully in the nineties, and during the Spanish-American War Congress gave him fifty thousand dollars with which to produce a man-carrying plane.

Langley built a craft that he called an "aerodrome." It was a "tandem" monoplane, which means that it had two wings, one in front of the other. These wings had a spread of forty-eight feet and the ship measured fifty-two feet from bow to tail. It was powered with a

Langley's Aerodrome, 1896.

remarkable gasoline engine built by a Cornell graduate named Charles M. Manley—a five-cylinder radial engine weighing 125 pounds and developing 52.4 horsepower, a remarkably efficient engine for its day. Two propellers located at the rear of the ship were to "push" it through the air.

The first attempt to launch the aerodrome occurred on October 7, 1903. The ship was to be sent into the air by catapult from the top of a houseboat on the Potomac, near Widewater, Virginia. The heralded event, however, ended in dismal failure. The aerodrome merely bolted from the catapult and toppled into the water. The craft was repaired and another attempt made on December 8, with similar results. Langley was ridiculed, and the American public decided that the idea of flying in a heavier-than-air machine was a nebulous dream of crack-brained inventors.

Yet, only nine days later, the self-financed and unheralded Wrights were successfully to fly a biplane at Kitty Hawk, North Carolina. The Wrights had the advantage of Langley in their superior knowledge of actual flight. They had built and flown gliders. They had experimented with methods of controlling the ship in flight by means of rudders and flexible wing tips. Before they ever applied power to their craft, they knew how to maneuver it in the air.

They made other flights on that memorable date in aviation history, December 17, 1903. Wilbur got into the plane for the second flight, rolled down the greased rail, and flew farther than Orville. Then Orville climbed back onto the lower wing and flew two hundred feet.

Finally, at noon, Wilbur stayed in the air fifty-nine seconds and flew 852 feet. When he landed, he and Orville gathered with their helpers to talk over those thrilling first attempts, and as they stood together in a group, the wind caught their plane, turned it over and over, and smashed it.

The brothers were not downcast. They had flown!

They returned to Dayton, built another plane, and in 1905 made a record of six miles. They sold their patent rights to France for $150,000, and in 1908, at Le Mans, France, Wilbur stayed aloft two hours and eighteen minutes, flew seventy-seven miles, and won a $4,000 prize. Aviation was definitely on its way.

In a recent year, about 2,000 commercial airplanes in the United States carried sixty million passengers between eight hundred cities on regularly scheduled air routes. Annually our great air liners transport

Culver Pictures, Inc.

Observation plane used in World War I.

large tonnages of mail and precious freight from one part of the country to the other. Aviation is a regular, important part of our transportation system, but the road it traveled to reach the goal of safe, dependable, humdrum flying is a story of heroism and daring.

Up to the days of World War I flying was experimental. Men built their own ships, hedgehopped until they knew how to handle the controls, then took their flimsy crates into the air. In 1909, when the Frenchman, Louis Bleriot, flew across the English Channel in a half-hour, his feat was heralded as epochal—and at the time it was. His entire ship weighed only five hundred pounds and he had fuel for only two hours.

World War I gave a tremendous impetus to the progress of flying. For air fighting, fast planes were needed. And they must be more than fast—they must have a wide cruising radius. Engines became more efficient—they developed more horsepower per pound of weight—and when the war ended, America had better ships and a large corps of young trained fliers ready to take aviation on to its next step, regular commercial flying.

Commercial flying in the United States dates from May, 1918, when the government established its first experimental air mail route between Washington and New York. The Post Office Department borrowed army fliers and army planes and set up its service, but soon found that between these two cities the air mail was no faster than the railroad. The planes could make only ninety miles an hour,

Flying the mail, 1920.

and the airports were far from town. By the time mail was trucked to the airport, flown to its destination, and trucked to the post office, a train could travel between the two cities.

Persisting in the belief that the air mail could save time, the Post Office Department established a line to Chicago and in 1920 extended the line to San Francisco. The distance to Chicago was seven hundred miles and to San Francisco around two thousand more.

Over these longer distances, the air mail proved itself. It could beat the trains. Emergency landing fields were constructed, and the mail tonnage grew.

The air mail took another step forward when night flying was inaugurated. In 1921 overnight service was offered between New York and Chicago, and in August, 1923, the mail was carried from coast to coast in twenty-seven hours, flying night and day.

Picture the pilot flying this first night route between Chicago and Cheyenne, Wyoming. For the first time his course was marked by revolving beacons. Great shafts of light, 450,000,000 candlepower strong, whirled like brilliant spokes over the dark earth, beckoning him on. Between these powerful beacons, smaller beacons of 5,000,000 candlepower charted his path for him. As he glided down for a landing, the field below him was illuminated with a thin sheet of light that hugged the ground so that it wouldn't blind the pilot's eyes.

Then, in 1925, the Kelly Air Mail Act was passed, giving the air mail business to private companies. Contracts were let to bidders, and the first commercial air route was born. The Contract Air Mail Route #2 was awarded the bid for Chicago and St. Louis and became the first private company to carry mail. One of the three pilots of the company was a young man named Captain Charles A. Lindbergh.

The profitable route between New York and Chicago was awarded to the National Air Transport, and from Chicago to San Francisco to the Boeing Air Transport.

The Boeing Company took aviation on to its next step with a

Aviation becomes popular. Curtis Field, 1925.

Culver Pictures, Inc.

Passenger plane of 1929, pilot's cockit behind and above the passenger cabin.

daring experiment. Instead of using the open-cockpit ships of the day, it constructed a new type of plane with an enclosed cabin between the wings, capable of seating two passengers. Behind the cabin compartment was an open cockpit in which the pilot sat. The Boeing company proposed to take passengers! It was unheard of, and others shook their heads doubtfully.

But Boeing pointed the way that aviation was to follow. It broadened commercial flying to include the carrying of passengers on regular time schedules, flying by night as well as day, and the modern air transport was born. When we consider that this was as recent as 1926, we begin to realize what giant strides aviation has taken.

It was in 1926, then, that the last link in America's transportation system was forged. Fitch and Fulton had given us the steamboat for our rivers and lakes. DeWitt Clinton had given us our canals. John Stevens, Peter Cooper, Horatio Allen, and a score of others had given us our railroads. Duryea, Ford, Winton, and their contemporaries had produced the automobile. Now aviation had arrived to add the element of speed to our transportation network.

From 1926 on, a series of sensational flights by Americans helped to maintain a white-hot enthusiasm for aviation. In May, 1926, Commander Richard E. Byrd flew over the North Pole in the tri-motored Fokker, *Josephine Ford,* with Floyd Bennett as his pilot.

Just a year later, the young air mail pilot, Charles A. Lindbergh, climbed into the Ryan monoplane, *Spirit of St. Louis,* at San Diego, California, and in two giant hops landed at Roosevelt Field, Long Island.

Already at Roosevelt Field were Clarence Chamberlin, with a Bellanca plane, and Byrd with his Fokker. A prize of twenty-five thousand dollars had been offered to the first man making a nonstop flight from New York City to Paris. Day by day the pilots scanned the weather maps compiled by the Weather Bureau from radio reports coming in from ships at sea.

On May 19, Charles Lindbergh decided it was time to go. It rained all that night, turning the field to mud, but the weather out over the Atlantic was clearing. After a sleepless night, Lindbergh got into his

Getting ready for the famous Lindbergh flight from New York to Paris.

Ewing Galloway

plane at the western end of the runway. The news had spread that he was going to start, and thousands lined the field. Byrd came up and shoved a weather report into his hand. The cabin door slammed shut and Lindbergh was alone inside, with a few sandwiches and maps for company.

About eight o'clock, May 20, 1927, his heavily laden ship began moving forward. He went more than half the length of the field before the tail of his ship lifted off the ground. Watchers held their breath, fearful that his ship was too heavy to pull away from the muddy field.

The wheels hit a bump and the ship was in the air. It dipped, then laboriously rose. At the end of the field, it just cleared a tractor and painfully staggered over telephone wires. It banked to avoid a hill and droned on, struggling to stay in the air.

All the way to Nova Scotia Lindbergh flew low to take advantage of the heavier air close to the sea. Reaching Newfoundland, he flew over St. John's to let people know that he was heading out into the Atlantic. Over the Grand Banks fishing grounds, darkness closed down.

At one in the morning, by his watch, dawn came. He ran into a storm and was unable to rise above it. Ice formed on his wings. At last he dipped down and skimmed a few feet over the waves, to check his drift by the whitecaps, and to get rid of the ice at the lower altitude.

The hours slowly ticked by as he flew with his landing gear just out of reach of the grasping waves. He saw no ships until he was near Ireland where he flew low over a fishing vessel and, cutting his motor, yelled down: "Which way to Ireland?"

Receiving no answer he flew by compass and in a short time raised the coast of Ireland where his passage was noted by men on the ground.

Darkness overtook him again as he reached Cherbourg on the English Channel and headed inland toward Paris. When he reached Paris, it seemed to him that LeBourget Field was too close to the city —it couldn't be the right place. He circled the Eiffel Tower once, decided that the lighted field he had seen was LeBourget, and coasted down to a perfect landing to find himself swallowed up in a hysterical jam of humanity.

He had flown alone the 3,610 miles to Paris in thirty-three hours and thirty-nine minutes.

So great was the world's enthusiasm over Lindbergh that what Clarence Chamberlin did a few weeks later was almost ignored. On June 4, Chamberlin lifted his Bellanca from Roosevelt Field with his backer, Charles Levine, as passenger. He hoped, he said, to reach Berlin. Over the ocean, his earth-conductor compass failed him and he was forced to use a secondhand compass Levine had bought at Roosevelt Field.

This compass was inaccurate and he could check his position only by chronometer. In midocean he flew over the steamer *Mauretania.* He knew when the *Mauretania* had left Southampton and therefore knew where its position should be and its direction of travel. So he flew along the length of it from prow to stern and in that way set a course for England.

He crossed Ireland and on to Europe where he encountered the worst storm of the year. He flew at twenty-two thousand feet and still could not get above it.

Exhausted, he turned over the controls to Levine and snatched a

In this plane Clarence Chamberlin flew nonstop from New York to Germany.
Brown Brothers

few minutes' sleep. As he slept, the plane got out of control and fell seventeen thousand feet before he could wake, reach the controls, and right the ship.

He came down through the clouds, identified the city of Dortmund, and set a course for Berlin. After forty-two hours of flying he landed at the little town of Eisleben not far from Berlin. He had flown 3,911 miles—three hundred miles more than Lindbergh.

In the years that followed daring fliers set one record after the other. We will mention only two. From July 15 to 22, 1933, Wiley Post, flying alone in his ship, *Winnie Mae,* circled the earth in seven days, eighteen hours, forty-nine minutes, and thirty seconds. On January 19, 1937, Howard Hughes, of motion picture fame, flew from Los Angeles to Newark in seven hours, twenty-eight minutes, and twenty-five seconds for an average of 332 miles per hour and a transcontinental speed record.

These deeds and others like them kept the American public in a state of high enthusiasm over the possibilities of aviation. Thus, through the period of trial and error, when regrettable crashes were bound to occur in too-great numbers, people continued to patronize the growing air lines. In 1926, the first year in which passenger carrying was done commercially, 5,782 rides were sold. By 1935, the rides had reached almost a million. By 1958, the number had reached fifty million and experts were predicting that this figure would be doubled in less than ten years.

As the popularity of air lines grew, designers everywhere were laboring to improve the airplane. To understand some of these improvements, we should know why an airplane flies.

Some day, when you're riding sixty miles an hour in your car, thrust your hand cautiously out the window and let the air strike it. You'll instantly realize that moving air can be a powerful force rather than a light, harmless substance.

The wing of an airplane, rushing through this same air, is thrust upward by the force of the air on the bottom surface of the wing, just as a skipping stone, striking the surface of the water, is deflected

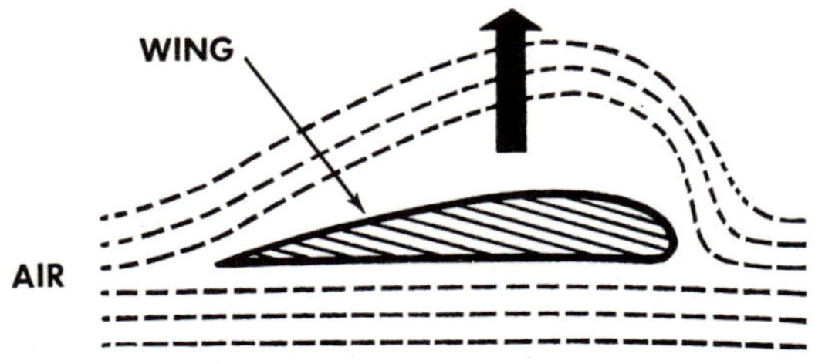

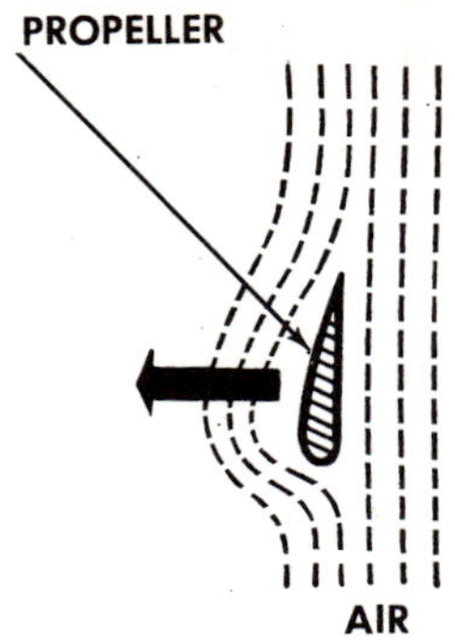

upward. But the air, in riding over the curved top surface of the wing, also exerts lift. As we have already said, when the flowing air rides off the top of the curve, it tends to reduce air pressure or, in popular terms, to create a "vacuum," which "pulls" the wing upward. Thus the moving air both tends to *push* and *pull* the plane up.

The propeller, driven by the engine, presents an angle to the air, and as it whirls it bores through the air just as a screw bores through wood. It must whirl tremendously fast to pull a ship through the air. Thus the propeller tends to pull the plane forward and the wing tends to lift it, and when sufficient speed has been attained the ship leaves earth and flies.

In the 1930's, to develop propeller-driven planes for the purpose of carrying men and freight, designers found it necessary to make engines more and more powerful and the ships themselves lighter and lighter in relation to their size. Every pound of weight saved meant an added pound of paying freight.

To illustrate the success of designers in building more powerful engines, compare the first Wright engine developing 12 horsepower with a radial Wright engine of 1938 developing 1,500 horsepower. Early in the career of commercial aviation, engines became marvels of reliability and precision.

To save weight, engineers used aluminum alloys, much lighter than steel, yet strong and workable. The efficiency of airplanes was further improved by streamlining. To understand the importance of streamlining, try to swing a broad paddle flatwise through the air. Then *slice* the paddle through the air and see how much more easily it moves. Blunt shapes encounter resistance in their passage through the air. Smoothly curved shapes, trailing off to a thin edge at the rear, move with the least possible resistance. Therefore airplanes today have become as sleekly and gracefully shaped as a rainbow trout.

The evolution toward this ideal was gradual. The small, closed-cockpit ships of the mid-1920's were succeeded by two larger transports, the Fokker trimotor and the Stout trimotor.

The two ships were radically different. The Fokker was a wood-and-fabric craft, whereas the Stout was the first all-metal ship to be built in the United States. Both ships were popular with the young air lines in the late 1920's, and the great debate of the time was whether wood-and-fabric or metal ships would prove most suitable for air transport.

The competition was suddenly and dramatically resolved on March 31, 1931, when a Fokker trimotor crashed and burned near Bazaar, Kansas, carrying to his death Knute Rockne, famed Notre Dame football coach. People decided then and there that metal ships were safer than wood and cloth.

This De Havilland carried mail between Chicago and St. Louis, about 1921.

The Stout trimotor was a solidly built ship with a corrugated skin of duralumin and space inside the cabin for fourteen passengers and considerable cargo. It cruised at ninety miles per hour and could take off and land at fifty. For a time these ships were built in Dearborn, Michigan, at a plant financed by Henry Ford, and therefore were known as Ford trimotors. They were also affectionately nicknamed "the Tin Goose." Ford trimotors are still in use today in special services where airstrips are short and a plane with low landing speed—yet considerable carrying capacity—is required.

The Ford trimotor wasn't fast enough to suit the demands of the coming air age, and it was soon succeeded by such new models as the Boeing 247, a fast, low-wing, two-engine ship with a retractable landing gear, and the Douglas DC-2. It was on these new and faster ships, in 1930, that stewardesses were employed to minister to the comfort of passengers.

Finally, in 1933, the air lines found the ship that was to set the modern pattern for scheduled intercity flight. This was the all-metal, two-engine craft known as the Douglas DC-3.

DC-3.

18 · FROM DC-3 TO JET

THE Douglas DC-3 is a graceful, streamlined craft with a wingspread of ninety-five feet, a length of sixty-five feet, and weight of twelve tons, loaded. It cruises at 180 miles an hour, about twice as fast as the Ford trimotor, and its roomy cabin can seat twenty-one passengers in comfort. Its price tag in the early 1930's was $125,000. (A modern jet transport costs about six million dollars.) Many DC-3's are in use today, both by air lines and private owners. They are readily recognizable on any airfield by the fact that they do not have tricycle landing gears and therefore sit on the airstrip with their noses pointing toward the sky.

It was in the DC-3 that the traveling public became accustomed to the refinements of air travel. The ship carried a pilot, a copilot, and a stewardess who served hot meals on a tray, offered you a stick of chewing gum before landing to help you adjust your ears to the change in altitude, provided you with magazines and route maps, and otherwise ministered to your needs. To the passengers of the 1930's, who looked upon an air trip as an adventure with an element of hazard, these touches of hospitality were a reassurance and a comfort.

With the DC-3, schedules were written that were to last more than ten years: Chicago to New York, five hours; New York to Miami, eight hours; Chicago to San Francisco, twelve hours. Compared to train schedules, these times seemed miraculous to the traveling public.

By 1938, when war clouds began darkening the skies over Europe, this country had twenty-three air lines owning 350 planes, most of them DC-3's, and scheduled air transport was an accepted part of our transportation system. In that year, the number of passengers leaped past the million mark and the air lines, in addition to carrying large tonnages of mail, were doing an increasing business in air express.

Businessmen were using air express to ship items in a hurry, such as newspaper photographs, printer's proofs, and machinery parts needed to restore operations in a factory. Health authorities were sending serum and medical supplies to halt epidemics. Newspapers were being air-expressed to big city hotels, so that the traveler could read his home-town paper at breakfast. Air lines were filling an important place in our transportation system by getting people and precious goods around the country fast.

In the 1930's, electronic airways were developed. In the old days, air mail pilots flew by reading a map and watching the ground and the horizon. At night, they followed powerful revolving beacons.

The pilots of the DC-3's were flying by instrument according to precise flight plans submitted to the dispatcher before take-off. If you had sat in the pilot's compartment you would have seen on the dashboard a maze of dials to tell a pilot whether he was climbing, diving, or banking, his engine revolutions, his air speed, his altitude.

The chances are that his DC-3 was equipped with a device called a robot pilot—more correctly, a Sperry automatic gyropilot—that automatically kept his plane in level flight, thus giving the pilot time for navigation and telephone communication. With the radiophone the pilot kept in constant communication with the ground, reporting his position, receiving weather data and flight instructions.

Through his headphones, the pilot was receiving directional signals that told him instantly if he were wandering off course. Above the station sending out these signals—called the radio beam—there was a cone of silence, and when the pilot hit this cone he knew exactly where he was.

All these advances—two-way telephones, improved weather reporting, electronic airways, better and more powerful aircraft—helped the air lines to establish safety records in the late 1930's that gave the public great confidence in their newest and fastest form of transportation.

During World War II, many of our domestic planes were commandeered by the armed services, and for a time all domestic air travel was conducted by fewer than two hundred ships. From 1941

Troop carrier, World War II.

Culver Pictures, Inc.

to 1945, the air lines had little chance to improve their service, but with the end of the war commercial aviation made a series of giant strides forward in size, comfort, and speed. During the war years, big, fast four-engined bombers, troop and cargo carriers had been developed, and these were now redesigned for civilian use. Larger and faster air liners succeeded one another at a dizzying pace.

The first of these postwar liners was the four-engine Douglas DC-4, which cost about a half-million dollars to build and could carry forty-four passengers at a cruising speed of 220 miles per hour. This handsome ship was introduced to the public during the years 1945–47.

The DC-4 was succeeded by what might be called our 300-mile-per-hour ships. There was the million-dollar DC-6, followed by the Lockheed Constellation, both of them capable of carrying as many as ninety-five passengers. Along with these four-engine marvels, the pub-

Special cargo-carrying airplanes became common after World War II.

Four-engined piston ships like this Lockheed *Constellation* introduced passengers to three-hundred-mile-an-hour travel.

lic was introduced to such powerful two-engine ships as the Martin 202 and the Convair 240. Hard on the heels of these new designs came the Boeing Stratocruiser, the first two-decked air liner to appear on the American scene. Its deep-bodied fuselage was divided into a large main cabin above and a smaller cabin below, the two cabins connected by a spiral staircase.

With these powerful ships the schedules had to be written all over again. It was now possible to travel from New York to Chicago in two and one-half hours, from New York to Miami in four, and from New York to San Francisco in ten.

Sensational as these developments must have seemed to the traveling public, they were merely a prelude to the most dramatic development of all—the coming of the jet air liner.

The big 300-mile-an-hour ships we have been discussing are powered by engines no different in principle from the 12-horsepower engine used by the Wrights in 1903. Both the tiny Wright engine and the big 5,000-horsepower radial engines on our modern transports are reciprocal gasoline engines, like the one in your automobile. Power is transmitted by pistons, traveling up and down inside of cylinders.

The jets employ an entirely different kind of power plant. The simplest way to explain a jet engine is to say that it sucks air in through the front, burns it along with a high-grade kerosene, and lets the hot, expanding gases escape through an exhaust nozzle in the rear.

Basically, that's all there is to it. The thrust of the gases escaping at the rear drives the airplane forward. To understand how this happens, blow up a balloon, then let it go. It will dart violently across the room, propelled entirely by air escaping from the small hole. The balloon—which is an extremely simple jet engine—is obeying one of the oldest laws in physics, which states:

For every action there is a reaction, equal in force and opposite in direction. The *action* is the air escaping through the hole. The *reaction* is the equal and opposite push that drives the balloon forward.

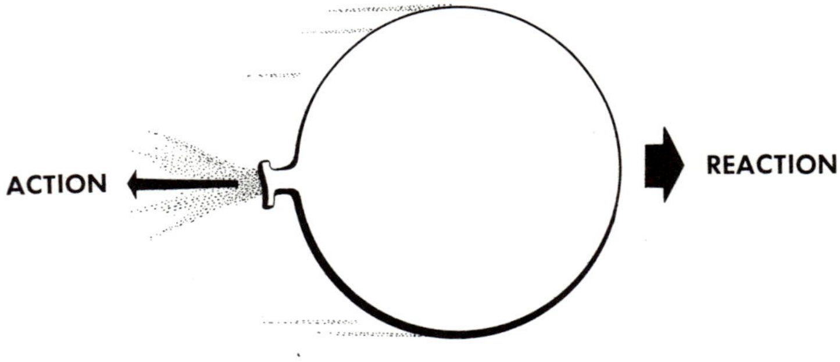

In the jet engine, the escaping gases perform one service as they go from combustion chamber into the tail cone. They pass through the blades of a turbine wheel, making it revolve—in exactly the same way as you can make an electric fan revolve by blowing on it. The turbine is connected by a shaft to a compressor in the front part of the engine. As the turbine speeds up, so does the compressor, sucking more air into the combustion chamber.

Compared to a reciprocal engine, the jet turbine is simple indeed. It has no pistons, no connecting rods, no crankshaft. It has no up-and-down motions—only turning motions. Air comes in one end, is burned,

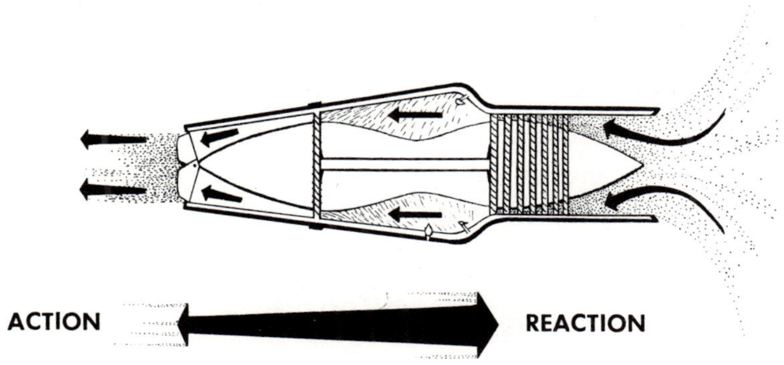

and escapes out the rear, turning a turbine as it goes. A glance at the diagram will show just how uncomplicated a jet engine is.

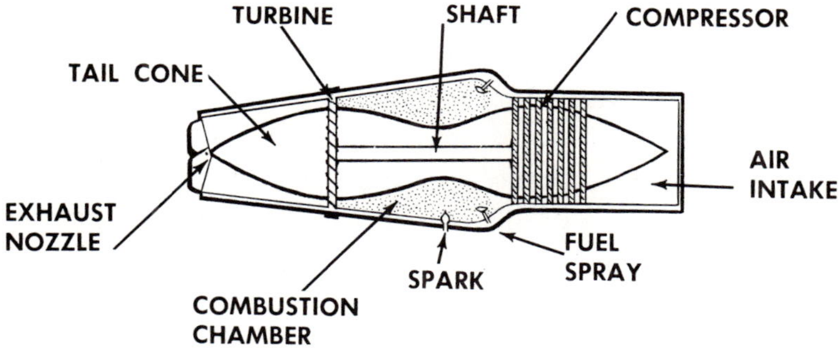

Jet-powered fighters were developed by England, Germany, and Russia during and just after World War II. The United States built an experimental jet fighter early in the war, but didn't enter seriously in the race, chiefly because its energies could best be used to produce conventional bombers and fighters in great numbers, for the Allies.

After the war, however, this country lost no time in producing such fighters as the Bell P-59, the Lockheed F-80, F-84 and F-86, and the big Boeing B-52 bomber. These jets saw service in the Korean War.

The years 1958 and 1959 may be put down as the dawn of the jet age for commercial transport in the United States, but by that time the European public had already been introduced to the high-speed jet travel. The Russian jet liner, the TU–104, had made its bow in

June, 1955, and by 1958 was making scheduled flights to many European cities. The British de Havilland Comet 4, after several years of experimental flight marked by tragic accidents in which pressurized cabins literally exploded at high altitudes, went into regular service in 1958, its cabins greatly strengthened.

Americans had been given a foretaste of what jet travel would be like when Capital Airlines bought a fleet of Vickers Viscounts and put them into service on July 26, 1955. The Viscount is powered by four Rolls-Royce prop-jet engines.

To understand a prop-jet (also called turbo-prop), take a look at the diagram of a jet engine shown in this chapter, and imagine that the shaft connecting the turbine with the compressor extends forward beyond the front of the engine where a propeller is mounted on it. The prop-jet uses the force of the expanding gases to turn a propeller, which pulls the plane through the air. In other words the prop-jet is simply a jet engine with a propeller added.

The Viscount prop-jet runs with less noise and vibration than piston engines and is faster. It hauls forty-eight passengers through the air at a cruising speed of 385 miles an hour, further cutting down travel time between cities. Its introduction provided a curtain-raiser to the age of the pure jet, soon to follow.

Pause a moment, to consider the advances aviation had made from the age of the DC-3 to the dawn of the jet. By 1958, this country had fifty-three air lines in domestic service, flying over fifty million passengers to 706 communities in 1,850 airplanes. Just twenty years earlier, our twenty-three air lines had passed a milestone by carrying over a million passengers in 350 airplanes. Traffic in two decades had multiplied fiftyfold.

By 1958 our air travelers had become used to four-engine monsters weighing about seventy tons loaded, cruising at three hundred miles per hour at altitudes generally under twenty thousand feet.

But they were now about to undergo an entirely new experience. In 1958–59, they would climb aboard ships that would weigh almost twice as much, cruise twice as high in the air, and fly almost

The Boeing 707 Jetliner.

twice as fast. This was a forward leap comparable to that from the lumbering Ford trimotor to the sleek DC-3.

The first United States-built ship to introduce these new thrills to the American people was the Boeing 707. If this big ship were set on its tail, its nose would reach as high as a twelve-story building and its wingspread would be almost as great. Loaded with passengers and fuel, it weighs almost 120 tons.

As you see it standing on the runway, waiting to take passengers aboard, you notice that the wings are swept back at an angle of about thirty degrees. This is a characteristic of jet liners. It means that the wings can be built thick enough to carry lots of fuel, yet will present a relatively thin edge to the air as the plane cruises along at its customary 575 miles an hour.

You note that the passengers climb aboard through two doors, the door ahead of the wing for first-class passengers and the door near the tail for "economy-plan" travelers. Depending on the seating arrangement desired, this ship can carry as many as 150 passengers divided between the two classes.

The four engines suspended below the wings look something like fat torpedoes. They have no propellers—only a big, open mouth through which the compressor sucks air. These engines are hungry fuel eaters. At take-off they consume kerosene at the rate of twelve thousand gallons an hour, but as they gain speed and altitude their efficiency increases until, at their cruising altitude of forty thousand feet, they will burn fuel at a modest two thousand gallons an hour. Even so, they consume fuel five times as fast as the big piston planes.

Jet liners need longer runways than conventional piston-engine planes. As the 707 gets under way, ingenious silencers on the engines reduce the high-pitched noise that critics felt would be objectionable to people living near airports. The big ship quickly accelerates to 175 miles per hour, leaves the runway, and shoots steeply upward at the rate of 1,200 feet per minute, trailing streams of black exhaust.

Within a half-hour, the 707 is cruising along more than seven miles above earth, high above weather disturbances. Outside, the air is thin and perhaps fifty degrees below zero. Inside the cabin it is warm, and pressurized to an altitude of five thousand feet. The passengers feel practically no vibration and hear little noise. When tea is served the surface of the liquid is unruffled. You can stand a coin on edge and it won't topple over.

On October 26, 1958, Pan American inaugurated 707 service to Paris. On December 10, 1958, National Airlines, leasing a 707 from Pan American, began flights from New York to Miami. In January, 1959, American Airlines began nonstop 707 service between New York and Los Angeles.

The Boeing 707 was the first of a line of United States-built jets and prop-jets that were to set new standards of performance for commercial aviation in 1959 and 1960.

On September 18, 1959, the second of the great United States-built four-engine jets was introduced—the Douglas DC-8—slightly larger and faster than the Boeing 707. On that date, both Delta and United began using the DC-8 on regular scheduled flights.

Meanwhile, in 1959, both the Lockheed Electra and the Fairchild F-27, two prop-jets, were introduced to the traveling public. In 1960, the Convair 880, a four-engine jet somewhat smaller than the 707, also began service on the airlines.

Thus, as we entered the 1960's, jets and prop-jets were taking over scheduled airline travel in force, and passengers were becoming thoroughly used to this quiet, swift, vibrationless kind of travel.

Douglas DC-8 Jet Mainliner.

If you wonder how these big new jet liners, some of them costing six million dollars, can possibly pay for themselves, the answer becomes clearer when you learn that one four-engine jet transport can carry as many passengers across the United States in a year as four streamliner trains or sixty highway buses. In transatlantic service one jet equals in passenger-carrying ability the ocean liner *United States,* which cost, by the way, seventy million dollars, or about twelve times as much as the jet liner. The jet liner can pay for itself because it can

Jetliner crews learn their business on this earthbound "simulator."

United Air Lines

make many more trips per year than any other form of transportation.

But aviation progress in the United States can't be measured entirely by the size and speed of its aircraft. The nation has also made great progress since World War II in extending air service to the smaller cities of the country. A few "local service" air lines began operations in 1946, hoping to win enough traffic to pay their way. In that year, they carried about twenty-five thousand passengers. By 1960, more than a dozen companies were carrying almost six million passengers in 300 transports, bringing air service to more than five hundred communities that had never enjoyed direct air travel before.

Helicopters, too, have been brought into our commercial network. These marvelous craft, with their whirling rotors for wings, and with their ability to rise vertically off the ground, hover in one spot, and fly backward, forward, or sideways, were developed into a practical airplane just before the outbreak of World War II, and have since been greatly improved in size and performance. They can now be built to carry as many as fifty or sixty passengers at cruising speeds of 150 miles per hour.

This helicopter seats fifteen passengers.

Heliport at West 30th Street, New York.

By 1958, three chartered helicopter lines were operating successfully. The first of these is the Los Angeles Airways, which began operations in October, 1947, carrying express and mail between outlying airports and downtown Los Angeles. Before long it began carrying passengers as well.

It was followed soon by the Chicago Helicopter Airways, which began its existence in 1949, and New York Airways, which started a freight and passenger service between the city and its three major airports in 1953.

These lines need no large airports. They can land on the tops of buildings or on small plots of ground called "heliports." New York

City's first heliport, located on the Hudson River between the piers where big ocean liners dock, measures just four hundred feet by seventy feet. Instead of runways, it has two circular concrete pads onto which the helicopters gently settle.

These three lines in 1960 carried 490,000 passengers and large amounts of mail and freight in a rapidly growing fleet of rotorcraft. A number of established air lines are now using helicopters to provide a "flying bus" service to other airports in our heavily populated areas. The future of our helicopter services seems bright indeed.

In other ways our domestic air service has been specialized to meet specific needs. Shortly after World War II, all-cargo air lines came into being, carrying only air express and air freight in all manner of flying boxcars.

The nearly two thousand airplanes, main line and local, of our commercial air fleet travel over a network of airways as clearly defined as our highways and our railroads. An airplane isn't permitted simply to take off and fly to its destination on a course and altitude of its own choosing. It must follow the invisible electronic paths of the Federal Airways System, a network 158,000 miles long connecting all the principal cities of the United States.

When an air line pilot starts his ship down the runway, he is following a flight plan that governs his exact course and altitude from start to destination. He cannot change it without permission from one of the traffic control centers operated by the Civil Aeronautics Administration. He is in constant telephone communication with these centers, receiving instructions and weather data. Electronic signals, showing up on his instrument panel, tell him if he is on course. As he approaches or leaves airports, he is visible on radar screens in the control tower, and the operator in the tower can tell him whether other airplanes are near him.

The impalpable air is mapped by the CAA all the way from the ground to the highest altitude used by air liners. You can visualize the air liner as occupying its own moving block of air ten miles wide, up to two thousand feet thick, and anywhere from fifty to a hundred miles long, depending on how fast succeeding airplanes are fed into the system. Following an accurate course in the middle of his block of air, the pilot can be confident that no other airplane will collide with him.

But this great airway system, seemingly unlimited in scope, is used not only by our nearly two thousand commercial air transports, but by our forty-two thousand military aircraft and many of the seventy-five thousand airplanes owned by corporations and individuals. The experts predict that commercial air traffic alone will double in the next ten years, and the authorities are now wondering if there's enough air above continental United States to accommodate all the people who want to fly.

Control tower at New York International Airport.
Port of New York Authority

NEW-YORK & BOSTON.

Daily Line, via Norwich and Worcester,

FROM

FOOT OF CORTLANDT STREET, PIER 18, N.R.

Old poster, 1855

19 · YESTERDAY—TODAY—AND TOMORROW

WHEN Washington was inaugurated President of the United States in 1789, men were transporting themselves and their burdens much as they had transported themselves since history began. They were using their own muscles or the muscles of animals. They could walk, ride a horse, or climb into a wagon. They could paddle a canoe or pole a barge. Only by sail could men avoid the sweat of muscles, and except for traffic on the Great Lakes sails were of little use in developing the interior of the United States.

Union Pacific Railroad

Mormon emigrants, 1847.

Settlers leading pack trains. Families walking beside wagons. Rivermen steering keelboats with long sweeps. A few established stagecoach lines in the East. Post riders carrying saddlebags of mail. A few coastwise sailing packets. Freight canoes and sailing boats on the Great Lakes. This was the transportation system of the United States in 1789, and it was little better than the Romans had enjoyed two thousand years before.

Then, within only a century and a half, man found new, swift, and tireless ways of getting around. The steamboat, train, automobile, and airplane arrived in quick succession. In the space of two long lifetimes, man improved his means of transportation more than he had in all the years since the dawn of history.

The United States and swift transportation were born together. By a wonderful coincidence, the steam engine and electrical power became practical when the country was very young. Because of that coincidence, a coastal nation was able to stretch across a continent in a little over a hundred years, webbing itself with highways, waterways, steel rails and airways, building cities, breaking sod, felling forests, digging mines, and carrying the fruits of its industry from one coast to the other by train, truck, canal packet, airplane, and steamboat.

Let's move Pikes Peak into Nebraska, climb to its tip, and survey the transportation map of the United States.

Take a look at the steamboat map first. In 1807, the tiny *Clermont* paddling up the Hudson. Four years later, the *New Orleans* churning down the wilderness of the Mississippi. Seven years after that, the valiant *Walk-in-the-Water* braving the sudden squalls of Lake Erie. Then more and larger boats, twin-stacked and gilded, loading iron at Pittsburgh, meat at Cincinnati, and cotton at Memphis and Natchez.

Glance at the muddy Missouri, winding up past Kansas and the Dakotas into western Montana, and you will see paddle wheels struggling through Indian country to Pierre, to Bismarck, then to Williston in the Badlands, and—yes—to Fort Benton in the Rockies, taking on loads of fur and precious metal.

Every year, more and more steamboats crowd the Mississippi and its tributaries until the number passes a thousand just before the Civil War. Then they begin to dwindle before the superior competition of the railroad, until today only an excursion boat or two, and a few showboats, remain.

But if the romantic steamboat is gone, its place has been taken by stubby towboats and businesslike steel-gray barges, each barge able to swallow twenty-five boxcar loads of freight, and more, in its ample hold.

The Mississippi River and its tributaries are booming. The channels of the Mississippi, the Ohio, the Tennessee, the Missouri, and the Illinois, have been deepened and marked, here and there dammed

Steamer on the Tennessee River going through the "Suck."

into long "pools," and along these charted and buoyed waterways, gliding intimately past hills, forests, and farms, are more than five thousand powerful towboats and twenty thousand barges.

Take a look at a typical tow as it pushes its way north from St. Louis. You see fifteen barges lashed tightly fore-and-aft and side-to-side, each barge two hundred feet long and thirty-five feet wide. Three abreast and five deep, they form a single expanse larger than three football fields. The towboat is fastened to the center barge with stout wires at the rear, a squat workhorse with two high "knees" of timber snugged to the gunwale of the barge, shoving the great expanse against the current at five miles per hour.

Inside the barges may be grain, coal, limestone, gasoline, or oil. But the barges may also carry automobiles, fabricated steel, or any manufactured goods that are in no particular hurry. Freight rates, by barge, are extremely low.

Let your eye swing, now, from the rivers to the odd-shaped cluster of the Great Lakes, an irregular expanse of water as large as the states of Illinois and Indiana, connecting the interior of the continent with the sea by way of the St. Lawrence. The tiny *Walk-in-the-Water* of 1818 has been succeeded by great ore, limestone, and grain carriers like no other ships in the world, long greyhounds that are all deck and almost no superstructure, serving the industrial heart of America with vital materials.

Between them, the Great Lakes and the inland waterways carry more than one-sixth of all the goods hauled in this country. And now the St. Lawrence, deepened to twenty-seven feet along its entire length, is bringing the ships of the world into the nation's center.

Let's take a brief look at the canal map. In 1825, there was the Erie, stretching out across New York state, carrying settlers to the Ohio country and bringing farm goods back. In the next twenty years, other canals in Pennsylvania, Maryland, and North Carolina . . . a fever of ditch digging in Ohio, Indiana, and Illinois . . . a great rush of activity, the shouts of teamsters, the gliding and bumping of packets and barges along towpaths—then the scream of a train whistle and the canal era fades.

Yet canals remain. The old Erie, now the New York State Barge Canal, is busier than ever, its power barges hauling millions of tons of farm products, ore, chemicals, lumber, and scrap iron every year. Train your telescope southward, and you will see from Corpus Christi, Texas, to Mobile, Alabama, more barges carrying oil, rice, lumber,

Childhood of rapid transit, 1835.

This is how our mail traveled west.

and grains along a chain of inland waterways and canals. And to the southeast you will see still other intracoastal canals along the Carolina and Florida coasts. Descendants of the famed Erie are busier than ever, serving the needs of a dynamic nation.

Cast your eyes back to the northeast to watch the spinning of the railroad web. See how modestly it begins with small, shiny lines at Baltimore, Charleston, and Albany. Watch these lines as they creep out, covering New England, stretching south along the Atlantic and westward into Ohio, Kentucky, Indiana, Michigan, Illinois.

A pause at the Mississippi as the Civil War breaks out, then see how the rails fling themselves across the continent like the uncoiling of a whip, winding and twisting through the Rockies over trails charted by buffalo and elk. Parallel tracks running westward from Omaha to San Francisco, from St. Paul to Seattle, from St. Louis to Los Angeles. Then north-south rails, binding the nation in a tight web of steel.

Over these rails you see first the tiny five-ton bugs of Phineas Davis and the West Point Foundry, hauling flimsy boxes and stagecoaches with flanged wheels at fifteen miles an hour. Then larger and larger locomotives, more capacious cars, and more luxurious coaches, until three-hundred-ton monsters of steam go roaring across the continent at seventy.

Santa Fe Railway

After that, a transition. The plume of smoke and the hiss of steam disappear from the landscape. The drawn-out *whoo-whoo* of the train whistle is replaced by the raucous blast of a horn. Silvery, low-slung Diesels shove the steam monsters off the tracks of the nation, and lightweight trains of stainless steel replace the heavy black trains of our fathers.

Laid out below you are 220,000 miles of track, still carrying almost half the freight of the country in spite of the mounting competition of trucks, waterways, and pipelines, still carrying one-third of our paying passengers in spite of the competition of air-lines and highway buses.

Let's turn our gaze on the highway map for a moment. In Washington's time there are only a few roads in the East, most of them dirt, a few of them bumpy stone. Going west over the mountains you can detect a half-dozen trails, being worn into primitive roads by the hooves of pack mules and the wheels of venturesome wagons. Then, early in the century, the National Road from Cumberland to Wheeling. A fine crushed stone highway to the West!

A brief burst of road building then—a few hard-surfaced toll roads that go into bankruptcy with the coming of the railroad. For three-quarters of a century our highway system sleeps until bicyclists and motorists raise their voices in protest. Then, a sudden revival. In one brief generation, macadam, asphalt, brick, concrete, and gravel ribbons go whipping across the country to the tune of earth movers, mixers, and steam rollers.

By the mid-1930's, we have a fine, surfaced network of all-weather roads a half-million miles long, but this proves to be only the beginning of a frantic race between our highway builders and our hordes of cars, buses, and trucks that mount year by year to thirty million, forty million, fifty million, sixty million—all demanding freedom to travel from one part of the nation to another.

Our highways are relocated and redesigned with more sweeping curves, more gentle grades, and fewer grade crossings to suit the higher speeds of our car-traveling people. We embark on another

Country road, 1900. *Culver Pictures, Inc.*

turnpike era, building four-lane, divided highways with limited access in Maine, Pennsylvania, New Jersey, Ohio, Indiana, New York, and many other states, and charging tolls for their use.

Then the federal government sponsors a great interstate system of main highways connecting all the principal cities of the land, a system 41,000 miles long, nearly all of it high-speed, divided highway, but free to the user. Today, out of 3,400,000 miles of highways and streets, more than two million miles are surfaced for all-weather travel, and still the construction race goes on to the tune of six billion dollars a year.

Rails, canals, highways, then the airplane. Down at Kitty Hawk, in 1903, a flimsy pair of wings hopping a few hundred feet over a sand dune. Here and there over the country, a few foolhardy airmen trying out their home-built crates in pastures. Then World War I, calling for speedier, sturdier aircraft. In 1918, a mail route between Washington and New York, followed by another from New York to Chicago. In 1926, cabin ships and passenger carrying. Then night flying, whirling beacons, floodlighted fields.

Ships cruising at ninety miles an hour . . . a hundred and eighty . . . three hundred . . . six hundred! Jet liners crossing the continent in five hours. Spacious cloud cruisers seating anywhere from forty to a hundred and fifty people, carrying more than sixty million passengers a year.

As you gaze out over the land from your Pikes Peak vantage point, there is one part of our transportation system that you may not see at all because most of it is five or six feet underground. Yet its network is nearly three times as long as the railroad network of the country, and without it the wheels of the nation would slowly coast to a stop.

This is our system of oil and gas pipelines, a system over six hundred thousand miles long, connecting producing fields with industrial centers, refineries, and shipping ports.

Sinclair Oil Corporation

Oil pipelines.

Oil pipelines had their start shortly after Colonel E. L. Drake drilled for oil in 1859 at Titusville, Pennsylvania. A few years later a wrought-iron pipe two inches in diameter and five miles long was laid to take the oil to a shipping point, and it was discovered that this little pipe could transport as much oil as three hundred teams of horses working ten hours a day!

Year by year, longer and larger pipes were laid, and, when oil was discovered in Texas, men were ready to bring it by pipeline 1,500 miles to the refineries of the Midwest.

Illuminating gas was transported short distances by pipe from field to town as early as 1821. When General Lafayette visited the town of Fredonia, New York, in 1825, he found his hotel room brilliantly lit by natural gas.

Sending gas long distances was difficult because of leakage, and not until 1891, when a satisfactory leakproof and flexible joint was developed, did the gas pipeline become feasible. Today, there are more than 425,000 miles of gas pipeline and almost 200,000 miles of pipe carrying crude oil, kerosene, and gasoline.

You can spot these lines if you look carefully. They follow the contour of the ground, climbing hills, descending into valleys, crossing under the surface of rivers, burrowing their way under highways and under farmers' fields, but every now and then they must rise to get a boost forward, and that is where you can detect their existence.

Along an oil pipeline you will see small, businesslike pumping stations, every fifty or seventy-five miles. These stations send the oil or gasoline on their way at pressures up to 725 pounds per square inch. Near them you'll usually find a "tank farm" where the oil can be sidetracked and rerouted to another part of the country. The tanks are interesting. They may hold anywhere from 10,000 to 150,000 barrels, are cylindrical in form, and the steel roof floats on the surface of the oil, rising and falling with the oil in the tank.

Natural gas is moved on its way by compressor stations located at about eighty-mile intervals. When it reaches its destination, surplus gas not immediately needed by factories and homes is stored underground in old mines, exhausted oil fields, and in those underground formations known as "salt domes." Some of it is stored in immense spherical tanks.

Few people, as they travel about the country, give a thought to our pipelines, yet they may be likened to a great system of arteries and capillaries, delivering power to all the muscles of the nation. If the flow in our pipelines were suddenly to stop, our cars and trucks would run out of gas, our homes and offices would grow cold, and the wheels of industry would grind to a halt.

From your vantage point on Pikes Peak you can see it all, gazing downward to our waterways, highways, rails, and pipelines, then tilting your gaze upward to see the thin vapor trails of the new jet skyways, four miles higher than the mountain peak itself. From a few miles an hour on our rivers and canals to six hundred miles an hour in the air . . . from a two-ton automobile to a fifteen-thousand-ton Great Lakes freighter . . . from a pipeline six feet underground to a skyway seven miles above earth.

This, in brief, is our transportation system today. What of tomorrow?

The highway race will go on. The great Interstate System will be completed so that we can travel from any city in the nation to any other and for the most part remain on divided highways with no grade crossings to slow us up. And when this project is completed, and when county and farm-to-market roads are all surfaced, nobody doubts that we will have to embark on still another and greater road-building program. We are as sure of this as we are sure that the seventy-five million cars, trucks, and buses that crowded the highways in 1961 will be increased by millions in 1971 and in 1981.

Our trains? The transformation to lightweight, streamlined trains will continue. In recent years, airplanes have taken the lead in carrying passengers between cities, but for distances less than five hundred miles, and for commuter service in heavily populated areas, trains are still the indispensable form of transport—and the safest. In the carrying of heavy goods, trains are the leader and will remain so, for many years.

Our waterways? As we write this, the St. Lawrence Seaway is in full career. The Missouri River is being deepened, so that the barge lines can push their way past Kansas City, Omaha, Sioux City, and some day to Pierre, South Dakota, and perhaps farther. Just as the Tennessee has been tamed with dams forming great reservoirs of water, so our other rivers will be harnessed not only for water power but for inland transportation. The boom on our inland waterways will grow.

Our airplanes? To many people it seems that the arrival of the six-hundred-mile-an-hour jet represents the ultimate in high-speed travel. Yet our experts confidently predict that passenger airplanes before very long will be able to fly at three times the speed of sound, or something over two thousand miles an hour. They tell us that supersonic passenger planes will be in operation in the 1970's. When that happens, San Francisco will be less than two hours from New York. If you leave New York at 8:00 a. m. Eastern Standard Time, you will arrive in San Francisco by 7:00 a. m. Pacific Standard Time. Beyond that, there's Man in Space, but this book is concerned only with travel in the United States.

Inside the control tower at New York International Airport.

Port of New York Authority

Ewing Galloway

A rotting canal boat in the dried-up Chesapeake and Ohio Canal.

The next time you take a trip over the country, keep your eyes alert for evidences of our transportation history. In Ohio and Indiana you may come across a long, straight, grass-covered ditch, its outlines softened by time, and you will know that you are looking at an abandoned canal—a shallow waterway that once teemed with loaded barges, straining mules, and shouting drivers.

Taking the B. & O., out of Baltimore, you will pass over a stone-arch bridge, the Carrolltown Viaduct, built for the original B. & O. tracks in 1830, and you will think of the days when a steam locomotive raced a horse—and lost.

Traveling the highway from Cumberland, Maryland, toward Wash-

Carrolltown viaduct.

ington, Pennsylvania, you will be going over the ancient National Road. You will pass stone inns, two and three stories high, that were built before 1820 as stopovers for stagecoach passengers.

West of the Mississippi, automobile highways follow the trails of Lewis and Clark, Butterfield's stage line, and the covered wagon routes to California and Oregon. The ruts made by the broad rims of the Conestoga wagon may still be found in our western prairies.

In the rolling plains of the Dakotas and the mountains of Montana, you will pass through towns—Pierre, Bismarck, Williston, and Fort Benton—where venturesome steamboats pushed their way, taking guns, clothes, hardware, and groceries to trappers and miners, and bringing back loads of fur and ore.

Here and there, mostly on the branch lines of the country, you will see a steam locomotive pulling a train of cars. Glance fondly at the high driving wheels, the plume of smoke and the cloud of steam, for it was these black monsters that tied the nation together with bands of steel.

In Cincinnati or St. Louis, you may still see an old-time side-wheeler, eager to take you on a river excursion.

The next time you are in Washington, D. C., go to the Smithsonian Institution to look at stage coaches, or the *Spirit of St. Louis,* and

Smithsonian Institution

consider the fact that this shiny little craft traveled nonstop from New York to Paris, thereby touching off the wild enthusiasm of the air age.

In Dearborn, Michigan, visit the Henry Ford Museum and look at the funny high-wheeled horseless carriages in which our grandfathers ventured out beyond the city limits, got stuck in the mud, and set up a clamor for good roads.

The story of our incredible transportation system is written in such sights as these, and, if you can read them, your next trip across the country will be rich in the kind of excitement that only a knowledge of history can give you.

INDEX

ABOUT FRANKLIN RECK

"My own travel experience began with a one-cylinder Rambler that cranked in the side and steered with a tiller. . . ." Since his boyhood, Franklin Reck has been fascinated by the various modes of transportation. He is the author of numerous books on the subject and serves as consultant to the publications department of the Ford Motor Company.

Mr. Reck studied at the Wharton School of Finance of the University of Pennsylvania and at Iowa State University. He was associated with *The American Boy* from 1926 to 1941, first as assistant editor and eventually as managing editor.

Mr. and Mrs. Reck live in Manchester, Michigan—on "7 acres of maple trees and garden, conducive to writing."

ABOUT AVA MORGAN

Ava Morgan studied art at Cooper Union and now designs and illustrates books. She is married to Alfred Weiss, a chemical engineer, whose work often takes them throughout the United States and Europe. When they are not traveling, Mr. and Mrs. Weiss live with their two sons in New Jersey.